Praise God!

WHO
CAN WE TRUST?

Sr. Mary Bernard SFCC

WHO CAN WE TRUST?

Sister Mary Bernard
SFCC

New Leaf Press
Box 1045, Harrison, Ark. 72601

Library of Congress Catalog Number: 80-80531

International Standard Book Number: 0-89221-075-3

TO THE

****   HOLY SPIRIT   ****

the

SPIRIT

of

LOVE AND TRUTH

May He convict us of our sins,
lead us to JESUS CHRIST, the
FOUNTAIN OF LIFE,
and to
our merciful and loving
FATHER IN HEAVEN

CONTENTS

ACKNOWLEDGMENTS

The author gratefully acknowledges the editorial assistance of the many people who read this book, especially the work of Carol Hoffman, June Boyston, and Joan Maloney in the typing of the manuscript.

PREFACE

Many people will wonder how a sister can write about sin in the world and of the flesh and the devil. Most people imagine that being a sister brings protection from the pollution of sin. But my vocation has exposed me to sin rather than shield me from it. As a teacher of religion to public school students of all ages, I encountered many drastic situations where only God could solve the problems. Whether I visited wealthy homes or shanties, I found people in spiritually deprived conditions. I realized the dire need for spiritual direction not only for my students, but for their parents also.

Teaching male and female prisoners and working in a "soup kitchen" for over two years also placed me in a position of responsibility before God.

This book is for anyone looking for answers in life. Some are facing dead-end streets; others are frustrated and bewildered at what might happen to our world in the near future.

It is for individuals who want a *love* that brings peace of mind, security, joy, and happiness in these days of fear, turmoil, and confusion.

Many Catholics and Protestants of various denominations are perplexed, wondering why life is filled with so many troubles which they can never overcome. Some think it is sufficient to be baptized as a baby, attend Church, and live a good life in order to obtain Heaven. I know many who are still involved in things of this world, the flesh, and the devil!

Others, through ignorance and lack of instruction, have succumbed to the plight of the average person today and have run into pitfalls in their spiritual lives.

These pages are in no way a theological dissertation, but a collection of thoughts and suggestions (and the Word of God) dealing with placing our trust correctly in our everyday life in this modern age.

Jesus does not want to send you away empty of heart and mind. He invites all of you, "Come to me, all you who are weary and find life burdensome, and I will refresh you" (Matt. 11:28).

SISTER MARY BERNARD, SFCC

CHAPTER I

It was a gorgeous autumn day in September in the heart of New York City, on the upper east side.

As my taxi came to its destination, I managed to dislodge myself with my crutches, together with the uncomfortable cast on my left leg. At the time, I was an out-patient at the New York Hospital and had just come from my weekly appointment en route to a savings bank. As I slowly hobbled to the door, I reflected how some years ago I was in the same situation in California—walking on crutches.

That first time I discovered an insurance policy better than any I had ever known before. In September of 1969 that policy completely covered a condition I had called degenerative arthritis of the spine. Now, four years later, I had to use the policy again.

After some manipulation with the bank's swinging door, I finally managed to get inside and wait in the long line for my turn. The woman in the front of me smiled as I approached her, and she asked, "Skiing, Sister?"

"No," I replied, with a bigger smile and a twinkle in my eye, "Mass—on the rocks."

With that answer, several people perked up their ears to listen to whatever explanation I might give.

"I fell," I continued, "during my new community's International Assembly last month at Narragansett, Rhode Island. We were preparing for a twilight Eucharistic celebration on the great rocks overlooking the Atlantic Ocean when it happened."

That explanation seemed to satisfy my intent listeners, but my mind flashed back to the particulars. Huge vigil lights were used, together with God's moon, to shed ample light for us when it grew darker.

Jumping from one rock to another before Mass, I suddenly came down with a thud, turning my ankle and seeing stars, and not the ones in the sky, either. The sisters came to my aid immediately.

I thought to myself, "I've been through a sprained ankle before, so let's brace up and try to get a seat as soon as possible." The excruciating pain persisted and so did my optimism. This was my third sprained ankle, I continued to reason with myself. I've walked on them before and survived. The last time this happened in California, I was all right the next morning.

After Mass, the sisters returned to the Retreat House, three blocks away. I held on to two of them, limping on the throbbing ankle. After much persuasion, I finally agreed to remain off my foot.

The following morning, I fully expected to be better. But God's ways are not our ways. His thoughts are not our thoughts. As I sat up in the morning, I put my left foot on the floor. It refused to receive the weight of my body. I was puzzled for a moment and then saw my Bible within hand's reach. I prayed, "Lord, please give an answer to this problem. You healed me once of a sprained ankle, why not now?"

The Bible opened to the Gospel of Matthew, chapter 12, verse 50 (for new Bible readers: Matt. 12:50), where I read, "Whosoever does the will of my heavenly Father is a brother and sister and mother to me."

I thought to myself, "Evidently this sprained ankle is the *permissive* will of God."

I must explain to my readers that God allows some things to happen to show forth His healing and restoring power. Some good examples are the story of Job in the Old Testament; the death of Lazarus in the Gospel of John, chapter 12; and the man born blind in John, chapter 9, in the New Testament.

This has nothing to do with the actions of the prince of this world, Satan. The evil one has control over those who do not trust and obey Jesus Christ and His Holy Spirit. We are either slaves of sin (and receive its consequences) or obedient children of God, made free through His blood on the cross and His word in the Bible. Jesus said, "If you live according to my teaching, you are truly my disciples; then you will know the truth, and the truth will set you free" (John 8:31-32).

Then I said, "Let's check another Scripture passage." I flipped the pages over, and I came to the first letter of Paul to the Corinthians. "Nor are you to grumble as some of them did, to be killed by the destroying angel. The things that happened to them serve as an example. They have been written as a warning to us, upon whom the end of the ages has come. For all these reasons, let anyone who thinks he is standing upright watch out lest he fall. No test has been sent you that does not come to all men. Besides, God keeps His promise. He will not let you be tested beyond your strength. Along with the test He will give you a way out of it so that you may be able to endure it" (1 Cor. 10:10-13).

Well, that settled that. It was the permissive will of God—and I was not to complain or grumble about it.

The next step, after getting dressed, was to get to an emergency hospital. The closest one was at Wakefield, a few miles away. With crutches borrowed from the sisters at the college, I managed to get to a car and was driven there to get x-rays taken, etc., to see what was wrong. I now realized this was no sprained ankle!

After the nurse took the x-rays, she commented, "What on earth did you do to your foot? Whatever you did, you mutilated it!"

The doctor was soon on the scene, and he looked at the pictures that told the story. "Sister," he said, "you have a fractured ankle, plus two fractured bones. I will give you an emergency cast, but you are not to go to any doctors until the swelling goes down in about a week. Then an operation has to be performed on your foot to have it set right before any healing takes place."

With all of this, I had to admit to the doctor I had no ordinary insurance that would cover the bills, no Blue Cross, Blue Shield—nothing. He said he would

16

send the bill to my address in New York City. Through the sister who was with me it was rumored about that I had no insurance. Some money was collected from a few sisters within my new community, "Sisters for Christian Community."

I managed, with God's grace, not to complain through the whole ordeal, three more days of the International Assembly. I even had peace in my heart knowing everything was going to be all right when I returned home. Being a self-supporting sister, I had a job as a companion in the evening to a wealthy woman in New York City. During the day I did volunteer work.

The long four-hour drive back to New York City seemed endless as I elevated my leg over the front seat. We finally arrived home, and the elevator man took my luggage to the penthouse where I lived. As I opened the door, I was surprised to see the cook greet me. She had the day off, and I was the substitute! The words of Isaiah 58:11 were reflected in my heart, "Then the LORD will guide you always and give you plenty even on the parched land. He will renew your strength, and you shall be like a watered garden, like a spring whose water never fails."

In the days that followed I managed to carry on my work as a companion, teach Harlem boys in a CCD class, handle an adult Scripture course, teach a class to criminally insane women, and continue counseling. The "soup kitchen" found me absent from morning duties.

When the bill came from the doctor in Wakefield, it was $82. The sisters had collected $86. Praise the Lord!

My next step was to visit the closest hospital as an out-patient. As the doctor finished the first x-rays, I asked him, "Doctor, when will the operation on my foot take place?"

"What operation, sister?" he asked. "There is no need for any operation at all. It will heal itself as it is now. But," he continued, "your x-rays show you have had a broken ankle on this foot before. No doubt the ankle will be weak in the future."

My thoughts returned to California where I had had my last sprained ankle, or so I had thought at the time. It had actually been broken. We had prayed, and it was *healed overnight!* Oh, the goodness of the Lord! I was reminded of the words of Peter, "In His [Jesus'] own body he brought your sins to the cross, so that all of us, dead to sin, could live in accord with God's will. *By his wounds you were healed.* At one time you were straying like sheep, but now you have returned to the Shepherd, the Guardian of your souls" (1 Pet. 2:24-25).

After five more x-rays and four different casts, the foot finally became normal enough to step on. Taking calcium pills and exercising the foot with considerable walking was the best preventative for any more ankle problems. Today, I have a wonderful left foot without any pain or limp.

The insurance policy I had discovered four years earlier was once again taking care of the problem. You see, I had been healed of degenerative arthritis of the spine at that time. I had had the arthritis for thirteen of the twenty-five years that I suffered with spinal ailments.

Through the recent x-rays on my ankle, I discovered that the Lord's insurance policy had healed a broken foot overnight that I had thought was only sprained. And now the Lord's insurance policy was about to provide for me once again, this time in a financial way.

A few years before, I had met a sister in transition (from her community to SFCC) who needed financial aid. I gladly supplied her needs, for I had a job that paid well. To my surprise, a few weeks after the hospital bill arrived, she sent me the exact amount of the hospital bill. Hallelujah! Now she had acquired a good position.

I mention all of this to introduce others to the insurance policy everyone needs. I call it the "**King's Insurance Policy**." It guarantees the policyholder **LIFE, PEACE, HEALTH, CLOTHES, ALL YOUR DAILY NEEDS, COMFORT, COMPANIONSHIP,** and an **ETERNAL HOME.** What more could a person need on this earth for security?

You may wonder what the premiums are. How wonderful to know that JESUS PAID FOR IT ON GOOD FRIDAY. All we have to do is accept JESUS as the LORD AND SAVIOUR of our lives. To those who accept the conditions of the above insurance policy, everything is *guaranteed!* It is through "REPENTANCE before GOD, and on FAITH in our LORD JESUS" (Acts 20:21).

Everywhere I go, I hear people being fearful, worried, fretting, and anxious about the present and the FUTURE. For years now, since I left my former community, the Lord Jesus Christ has taken *complete*

19

care of my financial, temporal, physical, and spiritual needs.

You, too, can have this wonderful peace of mind and heart in the midst of this confused and hectic world. You, too, can trust in God and HE WILL PROVIDE. This insurance is obtained by application to Jesus the King, Himself. *Ask, and you will receive the FAITH* that is needed to accept this policy.

It is the oldest insurance company in the world, having been in successful operation for thousands of years.

It is the only insurance company which **ensures against loss** in the GREAT JUDGMENT DAY FIRE.

It is the only company which **ensures against shipwreck** in the RIVER OF DEATH.

Its policies are **nonforfeitable**, never expire, and permit the insured to travel in all quarters of the earth, from the North to the plague-infected districts of China, India, Africa, and the islands of the seas!

It has **never changed its management.**

It ensures a man for more than he is worth. All applications must be made directly to the President. All genuine **policies are stamped** with a Blood Red Seal, which signifies Christ's blood on the cross.

It is absolutely **guaranteed,** for the "heavens and earth will pass away but my words will not pass" (Matt. 24:35).[1]

You, too, can have this same security that I have. **ABUNDANT LIFE IN THE NOW.** "God so loved the world that he gave his only Son, that whosoever believes in Him may not die, but may have eternal life" (John 3:16). "I came that they might have life and have it to the full [abundantly]" (John 10:10).

HEALTH: "He pardons all your iniquities, he heals all your ills" (Ps. 103:3).

CLOTHES: "If God clothes in such splendor the grass of the field, which grows today and is thrown on the fire tomorrow, how much more will He provide for you" (Luke 12:28).

ALL DAILY NEEDS: "My God in turn will supply your needs fully, in a way worthy of his magnificent riches in Christ Jesus" (Phil. 4:19).

COMFORT: "Do not let your hearts be troubled. Have FAITH in God and FAITH in me" (John 14:1).

COMPANIONSHIP: "Know that I AM with you always, until the end of the world" (Matt. 28:20). And, "Do not love money but be content with what you have, for God has said, 'I will never desert you, nor will I forsake you' " (Heb. 13:5).

PEACE: " 'Peace' is my farewell to you, my peace is my gift to you; I do not give it to you as the world gives peace. Do not be distressed or fearful" (John 14:27). And, "A nation of firm purpose you keep in peace; for its trust in you. Trust in the LORD forever! For the LORD is an eternal Rock" (Isa. 26: 3-4).

AN ETERNAL HOME: "In my Father's house there are many dwelling places; otherwise, how could I have told you that I was going to prepare a place for you?" (John 14:2).

I still had the crutches belonging to the sisters in Narragansett. How was I to return them, but through the mail? God stepped into that situation, too. The substitute cook, who stayed for some months taking the regular cook's position, knew the same sisters I borrowed the crutches from. They visited her on different occasions, and so the crutches were returned through her in New York City. You might say all this was just mere coincidence. I believe in DIVINE PROVIDENCE! GOD LOVES EACH ONE OF US and is concerned about us in every particular area.

But Jesus said, "No man can serve two masters." A person has to decide which one he is going to depend on. "He will either hate one and love the other or be attentive to one and despise the other. You cannot give yourself to God and money (at the same time)."

"I warn you, then," Jesus continued, "do not WORRY about your livelihood, what you are to eat or drink or use for clothing. Is not life more than food? Is not the body more valuable than clothes?

"Look at the birds in the sky. They do not sow or reap, they gather nothing into barns; yet your heavenly Father feeds them. Are not you more important than they? Which of you by worrying can add a moment to his life-span? As for clothes, why be concerned? Learn a lesson from the way the wild flowers grow. They do not work [this does not advocate slothfulness for human beings]; they do not spin. Yet I assure you, not even Solomon in all his splendor was arrayed like one of these.

"If God can clothe in such splendor the grass of the field, which blooms today and is thrown on the fire tomorrow, will he not provide much more for you? O weak in faith! STOP WORRYING, then, over questions like, 'What are we to eat, or what are we to wear?' The UNBELIEVERS are always running after these things. Your heavenly Father knows all that you need.

"SEEK FIRST HIS KINGSHIP OVER YOU, HIS WAY OF HOLINESS, AND ALL THESE THINGS WILL BE GIVEN YOU BESIDES. Enough, then, of worrying about TOMORROW. Let tomorrow take care of itself. TODAY has troubles enough of its own" (Matt. 6:24-34, emphasis mine).

A Christian, Jesus comments, has troubles, but is not weighed down or crushed by them. We do not have to resort to drinking or illicit sex to forget our troubles, or run away from reality by using marijuana, heroin, speed, or tranquilizers. We do not have to fear the future or be anxious about coming events in the world or visit fortune tellers or astrologers.

Real believing Christians have their SECURITY, TRUST, JOY, and PEACE OF MIND knowing that GOD LOVES THEM. He will protect and give them strength to OVERCOME THE WORLD, THE FLESH, AND THE DEVIL. "Come to Me, all you who are weary and find life burdensome, and I will refresh you. Take My yoke upon your shoulders and LEARN FROM ME, for I AM GENTLE AND HUMBLE OF HEART. Your souls will find rest, for my yoke is easy and my burden light" (Matt. 11:28-30, emphasis mine).

All through my life, even since I was a child (as seen in my first book, *I Leap For Joy*), my personal relationship with Jesus has proven to me that *He not only loves me,* but He *takes good care of me as well.* My work as a companion in the evenings, along with the volunteer work during the day, has ended. After I finished working on the manuscript of this book, God made me available as a guest speaker for many denominational churches, different Christian organizations, and various prayer groups. I depend and rely on God's almighty power and goodness, the mercy of Jesus and His forgiveness to sinners, and the love and truthfulness of His Holy Spirit.

HE LOVES YOU, TOO! AND WANTS TO CARE FOR YOU. TRUST HIM!

1. "The King's Insurance Company," *Silent Evangelist No. 54,* (Grand Rapids, Mich.: Faith, Prayer, and Tract League, n.d.).

CHAPTER II

Ever since I was a little girl, I have seen the effects of sin. As a child at home and in school, as a teenager in the glamorous city of Hollywood, I found the world, the flesh, and the devil in full display. Later, I was chosen as God's instrument and became a sister. Even in the convent, nuns are far from being perfect, including myself!

But, through it all, I had a Friend named Jesus who enlightened and instructed me as to the path I should take. In following Jesus, I have found something that I would like to share with you.

In reading these pages, I hope you will come to realize the love that our Father in Heaven has for you personally. The illustrations and warnings are from my heart, knowing Jesus can make you able to surmount your trials and crosses, if you go to Him and *trust Him*.

Our Father's plan for us was to enjoy life and never die—to live in harmony with each other without suffering or pain. He loves us so much that, time after time, He has extended His hand of mercy and forgiveness to sinful generations. But from the very beginning, man has failed to trust Him. Today we worry and fret about how things are going to evolve in the world's crises and in our own private lives. We desire security but cannot find anything in this world that can satisfy our hunger for love, peace of mind, contentment, and happiness.

It is beyond what the world can give us. In these days all hell is loose with hatred, violence, dishonesty, sexual abnormalities, etc. Immorality in the home and in social, business, and political life has corrupted society. Even religion has become adulterated with rules and regulations, pride, ambitions, and watered-down teachings of Scripture. The Lord asks, "Why do you recite my statutes, and profess my covenant with your mouth, though you hate discipline and cast my words behind you? Consider this, you who forget God, lest I rend you and there be no one to rescue you" (Ps. 50:16-17, 22).

It is evident that man is still searching in the wrong direction. Countries still trust in their own ultimate power, not only in their wealth of industries and technology and agricultural produce, but in their military manpower and arms of ballistic missiles, bombs, and massive navy and air force defenses. But, as history proves, all kingdoms come to an end. Jeremiah foretold this when he wrote, "Because you trusted in your works and your treasure, you also shall be captured" (Jer. 48:7).

Most people fall victim to the things of this world. Besides money, drink, etc., there is one very sneaky and subtle thing that has crept into our society. It robs us of communication with our family, of our time with God in prayer, of our duty to help others in need, and of the time to think about our destiny—heaven or hell. I have found very few people in the United States, no matter how poor they are, that do not have a television set in their homes.

All actions begin in the mind. What we see and read penetrates into our pattern of thinking and affects the system of values by which we live. No wonder the crime rate and illicit sexual indulgences have increased during the years we have allowed this worldly device to manipulate our lives.

Our minds, created by God, are beyond human comprehension, and yet they can be filled with only one set of values at a time. No person can know God in a personal way and still be filled habitually with the things of this world. Today, thank God, we have an increasing number of Christian radio and TV programs where the mind is elevated and the heart is uplifted to love God and serve our neighbor.

Years ago, a rich man asked his religion teacher what he must do to obtain eternal life. In response, he was told that the answer was in the keeping of the Commandments of God—do not kill, commit adultery, steal, lie, or cheat; and honor authority. After admitting that he had kept all those, he was told to become detached from the things of this world and follow Jesus. That was his stumbling block! Is it yours and mine, too? Is there anything such as human respect, self righteousness, etc., keeping us from an intimate relationship with Jesus?

It matters not how many past sins we have committed. He will take all guilt away, for "the Son of

Man has come to search out and save what was lost" (Luke 19:10). The first step is to repent—change your worldly ways of acting, thinking, and doing and *fill your heart with His love*. He wants to help us in our present circumstances. "Come to me, ALL who are weary [of this world's tinsel] and find life burdensome [with sin]. Take MY yoke [lighter than your own] and learn from me, for I am meek and humble of heart. Your souls will find rest" (Matt. 11:28-29).

An article, by a minister of God, commented lately that the temperature of most Christians is so low today that when one is a normal Christian, everyone else thinks he has a fever. Can we learn to be satisfied and not complain about things and circumstances in our lives here and now? Should not life become real for us and not like a part we play on a stage? Can we live before God without comparing ourselves with our friends and neighbors? Can we forget about our past life of sins and look forward to a future that has hope?

The answers can be YES if we turn to Jesus and change our way of thinking and our values in life. "My God in turn will supply your needs fully, in a way worthy of his magnificent riches in Christ Jesus" (Phil. 4:19).

The other day, I met a lady who had had dire needs in her life. She had lost her husband, and due to her reduced circumstances, her only child was so undernourished she could not even lift her arms. Knowing she was in a crisis, the woman turned to God and acknowledged her need of the necessities of life for herself and her baby. She then offered her child to God. The mother, not having finished high school, felt incapable of acquiring a paying position but implored Jesus to find her a job where she could help others in a medical way. Very soon after, she saw an ad in the paper wanting a woman between 35 and 45, who wished to be trained as a medical assistant in a doctor's office. She applied and was received for duty and training the following week.

Today her daughter is beautiful, talented, and in robust health. Now they have the necessities of this world's goods as well as the peace of living a Christian life.

Some people have reached the apex of what this world thinks necessary for happiness, and yet in spite of what they possessed, they have ended their lives in sorrow, tragedies, and even suicide. What more could a person want of this world's goods—beauty, money, talent, and the world at her very feet—than Marilyn Monroe and others in her situation? And yet, none of these temporal things could fill the yearnings of their hearts.

Jesus realized the temptations that would assail us in the material world. He reminds us, "No person can serve two masters. Either he will hate the one and love the other, or be attentive to the one and despise the other. You cannot give yourself to God and money" (Matt. 6:24).

Others trust their jobs! It is only logical that a husband would feel a sense of loss when fired, as has happened to so many men during these years of inflation. The news media has shown many families in situations where their children would not have the extra joy of gifts at Christmas time. Some parents added that Christmas was really only for children. What could they expect from a worldly custom? What a surprise they would have received if they had transferred their faith and trust to a living God who could supply their needs.

More than one child I know has been so *disillusioned* by the worldly customs of Santa Claus and the Easter bunny, that they refuse to believe in Jesus in later years. We may call it an innocent practice, stemming from the man St. Nicholas, but no person, not even a saint, has the prerogatives of God. He alone sees everything good and bad we do, not Santa Claus. Parents should realize that Jesus is the *real Person* they have to give an account to. He is truly alive today and longs for children and adults to *trust Him*. He wants to be part of our lives.

I saw a sign in a window last Christmas that read: Out of Christmas cards—only religious ones left! "To his own he came, yet his own did not accept him" (John 1:11).

If, during the Easter season and throughout the year, we could teach our little ones the power of the resurrection life in Jesus, what a difference it would make in their lives. We say this is all part of the culture we live in, and we cannot change it. I agree. Only the Person of Jesus can change worldly customs. "Don't copy the behavior and customs of this world, but be a new and different person with a fresh newness in all you do and think. Then you will learn from your own experiences how God's ways will really satisfy you" (Rom. 12:2, TLB).

Education is another of the top priorities in the world today. I thank God for the many people who have contributed to the scientific, technical, medical, and business welfare of our everyday living. But in all these advancements in our so-called civilized world, does all this knowledge and skill bring contentment and peace of mind? "Education is no longer primarily intended to teach mankind to serve God or to enrich life, but rather to give him a passport to the world of commercial scramble," writes an author who knew.

For some, business has become a god! How about you?

Competition for success in the world has snuffed out many men prematurely and unprepared for eternity through heart trouble, strokes, and other tension-related illnesses. "Trust in the LORD with all your heart, on your own intelligence rely not. In all your ways be mindful of him, and he will make straight your paths. Be not wise in your own eyes, fear the LORD and turn away from evil. This will mean health for your flesh and vigor for your bones" (Prov. 3:5-8).

If you want health for your mind, body, and spirit, never fall victim to the advertisements for beer, wine, or hard liquors. A salesman or owner of a product wants others to have or use it. This not true of the people who sell alcoholic beverages. When the owner of a liquor company is in an airplane or helicopter, he does not want the pilot to have the product within him.

He does not want to ride with a drunken bus or taxicab driver. He does not want to sail on a ship with a captain who is drinking. He does not want his wife, children, or relatives to become alcoholics—but he selfishly wants to sell to everyone else. He is in an ungodly business.

If you had the opportunity to work in a "soup kitchen," you could see firsthand just how evil the use of alcohol is. Men and women (people from all walks of life who innocently took a drink one day at a party, after work, or at home to relax themselves) have ended up on skid row. It was a little habit at first but ended in slavery! How many have I seen— very young, middle-aged, and old—who have died because they thought no one cared, or that there was no cure? Fortunately, some have heard the words of Jesus, knew He cared, and were cured. Praise God!

In Scripture, a wise man wrote, "O my son, be wise and stay in God's paths. Don't carouse with drunkards and gluttons, for they are on their way to poverty.

"Who is the man with bloodshot eyes and many wounds? It is the one who spends long hours in the taverns, trying out new mixtures. Don't let the sparkle and the smooth taste of strong wine deceive you. For in the end it bites like a poisonous serpent, it stings like an adder.

"You will see hallucinations and have delirium tremens, and you will say foolish silly things that would embarrass you to no end when sober. You will stagger like a sailor at sea, clinging to a swaying mast. And afterwards, you will say, 'I didn't even know it when they beat me up—let's go and have another drink' " (Prov. 23:19-21, 30-35, TLB).

It's the "in thing" to follow the crowd, to adapt to the social customs of the world, having a drink to "loosen up" at a party, at home, or the office. This has even crept into the religious sphere, where in some places, hard drinks are served for relaxation, recreation, and before discussion periods, so those at the religious retreat will be more open to express their opinions. Can Jesus abide in those who have compromised with the world?

Today, the majority of teenagers and younger children are following the example of their drinking parents and elders. One lad of sixteen said, "It makes us feel grown up when we cruise in our cars and drink and smoke. Besides," he continued, "it makes us forget that our parents are doing their thing and are not interested in us as persons."

How can we blame the teenagers for their indifference to the realities of life? They are searching for the security and peace of heart and mind that should be theirs while they are becoming young adults. Who will have to answer for them?

In the meantime, *alcoholism*, whether in the young or old, is causing 40 percent of all *hospital admissions*, 31 percent of all *suicides*, 60 percent of all *homicides*, and 40 percent of all *family court problems*. Alcohol is also responsible for 35,000 *highway deaths a year*.

Some organizations call alcoholism a disease, for some have biological chemicals in their body that make alcohol a poison in their system. But for the majority, it is an escape mechanism prepared by the devil to destroy the mind and the body, to say nothing of the marriages, homes, and the lives of the children. Only Jesus can help the alcoholic!

No man-made program can erase the sins of men. Only the love that God has given to him in Christ Jesus can *redeem* and put man back into his former image and likeness of God. His love is there for the asking. But the Lord God will never trespass the free will of man. He waits patiently and says, "Come now, and let us set things right. Though your sins be like scarlet, they may become white as snow. Though they may be crimson red, they may become white as wool" (Isa. 1:18).

"If we acknowledge our sins, he who is just can be trusted to forgive us our sins and cleanse us from every wrong" (1 John 1:9). We must realize that God *loves the sinner* at all times but hates the sin. HE LOVES YOU!

You may be thinking to yourself, "Well! Jesus drank with sinners. He even turned water into wine at a wedding party." I agree! But He drank with sinners in order to invite them into a new life of joy, fulfillment, and satisfaction with Him.

Jesus said to His critics, "I have not come to invite the self-righteous to a change of heart, but sinners" (Luke 5:32).

He performed a miracle at the wedding feast as an act of kindness, to change an embarrassing and difficult situation into a happy one. He'll do the same for you! He didn't attend weddings every day, nor did He drink every day! He was Master over Himself! Is He Master over your life and of your drinking?

"Stop loving this evil world and all that it offers

you, for when you love these things, you show that you do not really love [or trust] God; for all these worldly things, these evil desires—the craze for sex [or drinking], the ambition to buy everything that appeals to you, and the pride that comes from wealth and importance—these are not from God. They are from the evil world itself.

"And this world is fading away and these evil forbidden things will go with it, but whoever keeps doing the will of God will live forever" (1 John 2:15-17, TLB). When we live in Jesus, He makes us more than relaxed! He makes us free, with no worries, anxieties, or fears. Praise the Lord!

The Apostle Paul said, "Avoid getting drunk on wine; that leads to debauchery [sinful corruption]. Be filled with the Spirit" (Eph. 5:18).

Today I received a 1974 fifty-cent piece, and it still had "In God We Trust" engraved on it. In conscience, can we have it on our coins when we abuse the use of it so much? Gambling, with its lotteries, horses, bingo games, etc., is certainly *not trusting God*, no matter what the money is used for. "The end justifies the means" is not written in the Word of God. Our lives are not controlled by chance, but by God's loving providence.

"Stop worrying, then, over questions like, 'What are we to eat, or what are we to drink, or what are we to wear?' The *unbelievers* are always running after these things. Your heavenly Father knows all that you need. Seek first his kingship over you, his way of holiness, and ALL THESE THINGS will be given you besides" (Matt. 6:31-34, emphasis mine).

It is a distrust of God's providence when we allow chance to determine our gains or losses. "Keeping watch over riches wastes the flesh, and the care of wealth drives away rest. Concern for one's livelihood banishes slumber; more than a serious illness it disturbs repose.

"The rich man labors to pile up wealth, and his only rest is wanton pleasure. The poor man toils for a meager subsistence, and if ever he rests, he finds himself in want. The lover of gold will not be free from sin, for he who pursues wealth is led astray by it. Many have been ensnared by gold, though destruction lay before their eyes. It is a stumbling block to those who are avid for it, a snare for every fool" (Sirach 31: 1-7, Apocrypha Book of the Bible).

The other day I read where a forty-nine year old tycoon thought money was the answer to his happiness. When his security failed him, it led him to kill his wife, son, and himself in his fifteen room mansion. We can ask ourselves, what does it really profit a man to gain financial success, prestige, and power, if he loses his soul?

God tells us, "Fear not when a man grows rich, when the wealth of his house becomes great, for when he dies, he shall take none of it; his wealth shall not follow him down. Though in his lifetime he counted himself blessed, 'They will praise you for doing well for yourself,' he shall join the circle of his forebears who shall never more see light. Man, for all his splendor, if he have not prudence, resembles the beasts that perish" (Ps. 49:17-21).

The riches of Jesus will never deteriorate. His

Word in Scripture never changes. The promises that God has given over the centuries never fail. Banks may fail, the value of gold may change, but God always keeps His Word. Man's shortsightedness in his worldly materialism can never be equal to the wisdom of God in His care for His children. If only we would trust in His goodness as a little child trusts and relies on his parents.

Everytime I see a baby in the arms of his mother or dad, I am reminded of how God wants us to trust Him. The little one is not anxious, frightened, or fearful of the present or the future, as long as he is aware that mother or dad is near. Yet God knew the future times and said, "Can a mother forget her infant, be without tenderness for the child of her womb? Even should she forget, I will never forget you" (Isa. 49:15).

EVERYONE is invited to learn from Jesus. He, too, was tempted in all things. He, too, sought His Father's help and strength through prayer. Yes, all of us can learn daily at the feet of Jesus, feeding on His Word in the Scriptures. If we truly ask God, He will give us an answer; if we seek to find God, He will show us the way; and if we knock, He will open the door. How He longs to give us His love and peace of heart. "Peace I leave with you, my peace I give unto you: not as the world giveth, give I unto you. Let not your heart be troubled, neither let it be afraid" (John 14:27, KJV).

Many wonder why their lives are upside down, mentally and spiritually. They have time at home for the newspaper, worldly magazines, TV shows, and other entertainment, in addition to the hours spent eating, but *no time* to feed their minds with the truth!

Jesus puts it in concise words. "Whoever looks on me is seeing him who sent me. I have come to the world as its light, to keep anyone who believes in me from remaining in the dark. If anyone hears my words and does not keep them, I am not the one to condemn him, for I did not come to condemn the world but to save it. Whoever rejects me and does not accept my words already has his judge, *namely, the word I have spoken*—it is that which will condemn him on the last day" (John 12:44-48).

Since I have come to New York City, I have discovered the wonderful subway system. Millions of people put their complete trust in others' skills and talents when traveling by subway. We also trust our lives in the hands of the airplane pilot or the bus or taxi driver. Every product we purchase in the food stores calls for trust in the persons who are responsible for packing and selling it.

There are thousands of ways we trust one another in our daily living. Yet so few will trust the God who keeps everything in its proper place in our little galaxy, to say nothing of the millions of other galaxies! We take for granted the ocean, with its perfect timing with the moon, the sun that keeps its proper distance from the earth, and the world which keeps on rotating at the exact angles day after day for all four seasons.

We look ahead through each changing year
With mixed emotions of Hope and Fear

Hope for the Peace we long have sought
    Fear that Our Hopes will come to naught . . .
Unwilling to trust in the Father's Will,
We count on our logic and shallow skill
    And, in our arrogance and pride,
        Man is no longer satisfied
    To place his confidence and love
        With Childlike Faith in God above . . .
But tiny hands and tousled heads
That kneel in prayer by little beds
Are closer to the dear Lord's heart
    And of His Kingdom more a part
Than we who search and never find
The answers to our questioning mind,
    For faith in things we cannot see
        Requires a child's simplicity . . .
Oh, Father, grant once more to men
    A simple Childlike Faith again,
        Forgetting Color, Race and Creed
And seeing only the heart's deep need . . .
    For Faith alone can save man's soul
And lead him to a Higher Goal,
For there's but one unfailing course—
    We win by Faith and not by Force.

—Helen Steiner Rice

(Reprinted by permission of Gibson Greeting Cards,
Inc.)

"TRUST ME when I tell you that whoever does
not accept the kingdom of God as a little child will
not enter into it" (Luke 18:17).

CHAPTER III

I can recall several incidents in my life as a teen-ager that still excite me. One of them happened on an Indian summer day in San Francisco. I was in Lincoln Park, overlooking the Golden Gate Bridge on one side and the calm Pacific Ocean on the other. For hours I stood there, meditating on the temporal works of man, and then on the overpowering evidence of God's presence in nature, His majestic ocean. Time seemed completely suspended as I stood motionless in communion with my heavenly Father. I can't re-member any definite words, but—just being in His presence overawed me.

Now, the psychologists tell us that our environ-ment and childhood years with our parents have much to do with our thinking and behavior patterns in later years. I received very little demonstrated love from my father. But to me there was no comparison between the Almighty God, who could accomplish such wonderful works in creation, and my earthly fa-ther. God evidently gave me this spiritual insight from the personal love and friendship I had with Jesus since I was seven years old. Many things have changed in our world since then.

The typical American is perpetually caught up in the world's rat race of constant motion. It is either the club to attend, committees and boards to be on, educational or cultural courses to be enrolled in, entertainments to enjoy, TV to watch, and books to read or it is the business, home, or school work to be accomplished. No wonder tranquilizers are the biggest selling product in America today. Our minds are so absorbed with things to do, places to go, and work to be done! Is there any room left for the brain to really rest, relax, and think?

On the other side of the coin is the pitiful state of the elderly folk who live alone or in rest homes. Most semi-retired people have nothing much on their minds and little to do. The asylums and hospitals are filled with thousands who have become vegetables, where the sick lie for months and years, without hope of returning to society. The typical American has no time to think and the old folk, too much.

The majority of men and women I have spoken to seem to think God is just too busy to bother with their problems and difficulties. He seems totally abstract to many church goers, and they feel He has no power to help them and is not concerned about their daily needs and hopes. They question, "How can God be interested in me? How can He give His love to a miserable and sinful person such as I am?"

This is just the reason why a person should get to know God, the heavenly Father, in a personal way. HE DOES LOVE YOU! He has fashioned this universe, this world, from formless matter and made it a home for YOU. He has, in spite of the evil that has come into it through Satan, made provision for *forgiveness of sins* through *His Son Jesus,* who died for *all of us.* God loves all things, including you. What He hated He would not have fashioned. And how could a thing remain, unless God willed it and preserved it. God, the lover of souls, has placed His imperishable spirit in all human beings, in all things that have life.

There are some who have the opportunity to dwell on the marvels of creation, the unfathomable workmanship of God's *unseen actions* in the natural world, for example:

1. The biologist comes into contact with microorganisms, living things too small to be seen with the naked eye, that are found in great numbers in the air, soil, and water.

2. The meteorologist studies and gives reports on the atmosphere and the weather.

3. The nuclear physicist delves into the components, structure, and behavior of the nucleus of the atom.

4. The electronics experts have revolutionized our modern society, bringing to the mass media: radio, short wave, and TV and the communications of telephone, telegraph, etc. Besides these, they have developed the electrical machines, appliances, and gadgets that fill our homes, offices, schools, and industrial plants. Many things these people work with are invisible to the naked eye, but we know they exist because of their effects in and on our everyday lives.

The "scientific explosion" is a phenomenon of this age. More scientific progress has been made in the last fifty years than during the preceding five thousand years. In fact, over ninety percent of the scientists the world has ever produced are alive today. Everywhere we see dramatic evidence of the breathtaking scope of man's inventive genius. And yet, wherever man probes in his scientific investigation, he finds that God has a prior claim to originality.

Consider the astronauts who brought the moon closer to us through their exploration and the Viking spacecraft that landed on Mars July 20, 1976, and sent back pictures of the planet's surface. We now know more about our vast solar system which holds our galaxy and its nine planets, asteroids, satellites, and numerous comets.

But what kind of a King is our God? Intelligent? Look at the plan, not only of our little galaxy, but of the multiplied millions of galaxies in space. Personal? We know this because He has communicated with us by becoming the man, Jesus Christ. He has revealed to us, in a life identifiably human and unmistakably divine, that the true nature of God is LOVE. "When I behold Your heavens and the work of Your fingers, the moon and the stars which You hold in place— What is man that You should be mindful of him?" (Ps. 8:4-5).

How very few of us think of our earth, of how it was created through the past millenniums. The geologic eras have baffled man as to the time and formation of the earth, its land and seas, its mineral deposits and the growth of simple marine life, algae, the fish and animal life of vertebrates, which stagger the mind in their variety.

Another of God's mysteries is the plant kingdom, which man could not do without. It is essential to the balance of nature and in the life of man. Only green plants can perform photosynthesis which is the ultimate source of oxygen and food for all animals.

Last, but not least, is the creation of the human body with its complex structure and functions. The study of each human part could take an intelligent person's lifetime.

There are many parts we could consider, but we'll take the two most important. First, the brain, man's own computer, was able to conceive the electronic computer. But who conceived the brain? It was designed for specific functions. The cranium encloses the center of the entire nervous system: the cerebrum which controls our consciousness, sensations, and our voluntary actions; the cerebellum which coordinates the muscular activity; and the medulla oblongata, which controls all involuntary activity and connects the brain with the spinal cord. If the brain did not function dependably, as it does, then thinking would just "happen" and thus would be unreliable. Words like "cause," "effect," and "logic" would be meaningless. Consequently, there must be a prior claim to design that could come only from God Himself.

Second is the heart, our mechanical pump. What machine can compare with the human heart, which pumps blood through the entire body one hundred thousand times every day? It has the work expectancy of seventy years or more, if the person eats and lives right. What other machine can work this way without a shutdown for maintenance or repair? Who designed the heart?

Only a loving God could, from a sperm and an egg, form a rational being who can see, think, hear, speak, feel, and move.

From the mind, heart, and soul comes the beautiful work of the artist who has the ability to depict objects, scenes, or people that almost come to life; from it comes the genius of the composer who creates the melodious notes and chords of music; and from it comes the talent of the poet who fashions words and expressions into vivid imagery of fantasy and truth.

"From the heaven the LORD looks down; he sees all mankind. From His fixed throne he beholds all who dwell on the earth. He who fashioned the heart of each, he who knows all their works" (Ps. 33: 13-15).

Finally, the incredible varieties of clothing and foodstuffs that God provides us demonstrates His intention to fulfill all our needs. Only man has put the stumbling block of selfishness and sin in the way that prevents the flow of His goodness from giving us all our needs.

The above are examples of how God shows His mercy and compassion and love for us in a natural way. Few people stop to think of them, their origin, or their Maker. It is due to the Lord's tenderness that we are not consumed for our ingratitude. Still, His forgiveness does not fail. "I, the LORD, alone probe the mind and test the heart, to reward everyone according to his ways, according to the merit of his deeds" (Jer. 17:10).

We have looked at some of the natural gifts God has given us, but they could never be compared to His spiritual ones! "How deep are the riches and the wisdom and the knowledge of God! How inscrutable his judgments, how unsearchable his ways! For 'who has known the mind of the Lord? Or who has been his counselor? Who has given him anything so as to deserve return?' For from him and through him and for him all things are. To him be glory forever" (Rom. 11:33-36).

All people grow physically if they protect and replenish themselves with God's natural gifts of clothing, food, water, air, and shelter, and if they get sufficient exercise. They grow mentally if they expand their intellectual capacity. But all too many remain spiritual infants or are stunted in their spiritual growth.

I have met thousands who have attended parochial or private denominational schools for eight, twelve, or sixteen years and are spiritual dwarfs. WHY? It was not because of any school's academic rating, but was due to the teachers' and/or students' inability to accept Jesus on a personal level.

Before anyone can become a Christian, he must realize Jesus is a PERSON and not just a biblical historical character. So many merely know ABOUT JESUS, rather than personally knowing Jesus; consequently they feel He is dead in their own lives.

I remember visiting a family not so long ago in Flushing, Queens, New York. During dinner, the twenty year old son exclaimed to me, "You talk as if Jesus was a REAL PERSON."

"He surely is," I replied, "and He LOVES YOU

personally. You can accept Him, too, as your Saviour and have a new fulfilled life."

"Whoever believes [has faith in and trusts and obeys] in the Son has life eternal. Whoever disobeys [rejects] the Son will not see life, but must endure the wrath of God" (John 3:36).

Our personal contact with God in prayer must be nourished and replenished with His Word and His love, just as our body is nourished by eating food and our mind is fed by constructive thoughts. "Not on bread alone is man to live, but on every utterance that comes from the mouth of God" (Matt. 4:4).

Years ago there was a commercial advertisement for Packard cars. It read, "Ask the man who owns one." Truthfully, this motto can be transferred into a spiritual maxim—ask the person who has accepted Jesus into his life and you will find a transformed one.

God is LOVE. This is His everlasting gift to us, a gift that surpasses all understanding. "God so loved the world that *he gave* his only Son, that whoever believes [trusts and relies] in him, may not die but may have eternal life" (John 3:16).

God did not send His Son Jesus into the world to condemn it, but to save those who are lost. Those who believe and confide in Jesus don't feel judged. With this in mind, all fear of death and judgment are gone. Our security, happiness, and peace of mind are not dependent on what we accomplish in this life or on the possessions we have. Our security comes from trusting in our loving God, Who is unchangeable and everlasting and loves us personally. There are many spiritual promises in God's Word. All come true if we trust in and rely on Him. Heaven and earth may pass away, but His Words will never pass away.

This does not mean that God neglects to punish the wicked and those who reject Him. Jesus pointed this out very strongly in His story of Dives and Lazarus in Luke 16:19-31. If you notice, the rich man who went to hell did no harm to anyone. But he did neglect to love God and his neighbor.

The poor man, Lazarus, suffered much hardship, poverty, and sickness in this life for a short time but had no bitterness or complaints. What a contrast in their ultimate reward and punishment. Nothing could change the condition of either one after death. We have only one chance, only one test in this present life! God wants us to pass the eternal examination. He finds no pleasure in punishment, but He is just and shows no partiality to anyone.

Only in God can a soul be at rest. From Him comes all hope. He is our Rock, our strength, and our salvation. If the Lord is the Head of your home, then it will stand, no matter how terrible the storm. If He is not the Head of your household, *step out in faith in prayer; you will find Him.*

"Seek the LORD while he may be found, call him while he is near. Let the scoundrel forsake his way, and the wicked man his thoughts. Let him turn to the LORD for mercy; to our God, who is generous in forgiving. 'For my thoughts are not your thoughts, nor are your ways my ways,' says the LORD" (Isa. 55:6-8). Walk with God. Live in His Word, yield your life to Jesus, and He will bear your burdens.

I read something the other day which I would

like to share with you, and I hope the words sink
deeply into your heart and mind.

> Today, upon a bus, I saw a lovely girl with
>   golden hair,
> Envied her, she seemed so happy and I
>   wished I were as fair,
> When suddenly she rose to leave, I saw her
>   hobble down the aisle;
> She had one leg and wore a crutch; and as
>   she passed, a smile.
>> Oh, God, forgive me when I whine,
>> I have two legs; the world is mine.
> And then I stopped to buy some sweets.
> The lad who sold them had such charm,
> I talked with him, he seemed so glad,
> If I were late, 'twould do no harm;
> And as I left he said to me, "I thank you
>   sir, you have been so kind.
> It's nice to talk with folks like you; you
>   see," he said, "I am blind."
>> Oh, God, forgive me when I whine,
>> I have two eyes, the world is mine.
> Later, walking down the street, I saw a girl
>   with eyes of blue.
> She stood and watched the others play;
> It seemed she knew not what to do,
> I stopped a moment, then I said,
> "Why don't you join the others, dear?"
> She looked ahead without a word.
> And then I knew she could not hear.
>> Oh, God, forgive me when I whine,

I have two ears, the world is mine.
With legs to take me where I'd go.
With eyes to see the sunset glow.
With ears to hear what I would know.
Oh, God, forgive me when I whine!
I have YOU, and the world is mine.

—Anonymous

We have so many wonderful natural gifts to be thankful for in this life.

There are also many times when we do not recognize God's spiritual gifts. When we are harassed or plagued with tragedies that come into our lives, we resort to Him as our last hope. And all along, He has been waiting for us. I met a man recently who had lost his wife and three children in a car accident, while he survived to become an alcoholic. After five years of trying everything in order to forget his sorrow, he tried God.

He had seen the difference in some of his friends. They, too, had had extreme trials and found Jesus! This means, that "If anyone is in Christ, he is a new creation. The old order has passed away; now all is new!" (2 Cor. 5:17).

In my own life I found much peace of mind when I realized that God truly loved me no matter what He permitted to happen to me. For twenty-five years I was afflicted with a spine ailment. It did not curtail my teaching assignments until the very end, but it did bring about situations where I had to rely exclusively on God. Many times His presence seemed to disappear. It was on two such occasions that my faith grew in tremendous proportions: after the degenerative arthritis of the spine forced me to use crutches, and when I discovered I would be a bedridden patient for life.

All the while, I thought this suffering was my ticket to heaven, until a wonderful lady came to see me. June met me in a rest home where months before I had had to resort to a wheelchair in order to visit the patients. She explained to me that Jesus never made anyone sick or crippled in His ministry here on earth. God, in His great love for us, sent His Son, Jesus, to be on earth, not only to nail our sins to the cross, but also that through His sufferings, we could be healed!

June pointed out two Scripture passages for me. The first was in Peter's epistle, "In his own body he brought your sins to the cross, so that all of us, dead to sin, could live in accord with God's will. By his wounds you were healed" (1 Pet. 2:24). The second scripture was in the fifty-third chapter of Isaiah concerning the Suffering Servant [Jesus], "But he was pierced for our offenses, crushed for our sins; Upon him was the chastisement *that makes us whole,* by *his stripes we were healed"* (Isa. 53:5).

It was through the scriptures and through the lady's prayers for me that only two days later, in September, 1969, Jesus' resurrection power brought me a wonderful healing. I have been able to be on my feet ever since. Thank God for His great mercy and compassion toward me. His Words are true, "Make straight the paths you walk on, that your halting limbs may not be dislocated but healed" (Heb. 12:13).

I can say with the Psalmist, "I will praise the Lord no matter what happens. I will constantly speak of his glories and grace. I will boast of all his kindness to me. Let all who are discouraged take heart. Let us praise the Lord together, and exalt his Name.

"For I cried to him and he answered me! He freed me from all my fears. Others too were radiant at what he did for them. Theirs was no downcast look of rejection! This poor man cried to the Lord—and the Lord heard him and saved him out of his troubles. For the Angel of the Lord guards and rescues all who reverence him.

"Oh, put God to the test and see how kind he is! See for yourself the way his mercies shower down on all who TRUST IN HIM. If you belong to the Lord, reverence him; for everyone who does this has everything he needs. . . . The Lord is close to those whose hearts are breaking; he rescues those who are humbly sorry for their sins. The good man does not escape all troubles—he has them too. But the Lord helps him in each and every one" (Ps. 34:1-9, 18, 19, LB).

Not long ago I was introduced to a young lady who also realizes the wonderful mercy and goodness of God. In a Catholic grammar school, she was not told of Satan's new tactics in the drug world. Upon entering a public high school, she was confronted with persons who gave her new things to try. Naively, she did. Before long she was addicted to marijuana and gradually to heroin; soon she was mainlining.

Eventually, her plight worsened until she was sleeping in doorways, empty cars, etc., and finally she was behind prison bars. In time, she decided to return home, tell her parents, and obtain help.

Not long after, a lighted match set fire to her beautiful long hair and she was wholly enveloped in flames. Forty percent of her body was covered with third degree burns. She was taken to the hospital practically dead; her sight, hearing, and speech were also gone. After being anointed twice by a priest, they waited for her death. Instead, they witnessed her sitting up in bed and saying, "I saw God." It was then that everyone present thought it was all over. The nurse, though, caught signs of life and realized her vision, speech, and hearing had returned, as well as normal breathing.

Today, this young lady has a beautiful face and hardly any scars on her body. She relates how she saw God in her vision and asked Him if she could return to earth and suffer for her past sins. The Lord denied the request, but she was told to return and give glory to her Maker.

Time is no element in the works of God. In His eyes one day is as a thousand years! "The Lord does not delay in keeping his promise—though some consider it 'delay.' Rather, he shows you generous patience, since he wants none to perish but all to come to repentance" (2 Pet. 3:9).

We do not realize, nor can we grasp, God's tremendous power or concern for each individual in the world, no matter what culture, race, circumstances or time they live in. Job, for instance, was a non-Jew, before Christ's time, yet what lessons we can learn from his faith and trust in God.

Very few experience the trials Job endured! God permitted Satan to test and afflict him! While he lost his possessions and his children and was afflicted in his own body and discouraged by everyone, Job never complained or cursed God.

He said, "Though he slay me, yet will I trust in him" (Job 13:15, KJV).

Job knew his innocence, but did not know why he was afflicted. Calling out to God, he received his reply. It was not one of explanation, but an insight to God's mighty power and omniscience.

God's questions to Job (a few related here) might easily be reviewed and pondered in our own minds when we question His providence in our lives. "Are you using your ignorance to deny My providence? Where were you when I laid the foundation of the earth? Tell me if you know so much. Do you know how its dimensions were determined and who did the surveying? Who decreed the boundaries of the seas, when they gushed from the depths? Has the location of the gates of death been revealed to you? Can you hold back the stars? Who gives intuition and instinct?" (Job 38).

And on and on the questions continued until God asked, "Will you yield? Do God's critics have the answers? Are you going to discredit my justice and condemn me, so that you say you're right? Are you as strong as God and can shout as loudly as he?" (Job 40:2, 9).

Hopefully you and I will respond as Job did. "You ask who it is who has so foolishly denied your providence. It is I" (Job 42:3, LB).

But why wait for some catastrophe to happen? Why not be prepared to meet the trials, sorrows, and circumstances of life, *by taking time out each day to know God personally.* He is the *only ONE* Who can be of help in the day of trouble.

Most people think of God as Someone in the sky Who provides, or does not provide, for their temporal and spiritual needs. Do you give Him an opportunity to prove Himself? Do you ever think of letting Him control your life? Do you sit down everyday and *read and reflect on His Word?* Do you take time out and *reflect deeply on His great love for you?* How He longs for you to listen to His voice, but—you are much too busy! His voice can be heard only in the quiet of our minds and our hearts.

Just close your eyes and open your heart
And feel your worries and cares depart.
Just yield yourself to the Father above,
And let Him hold you secure in His love.
For life on earth grows more involved
With endless problems that can't be solved.
But God only asks us to do our best.
Then He will "take over" and finish the rest.
So when you are tired, discouraged and blue,
There's always one door that is open for you.
And that is the door to the house of prayer
And you'll find God waiting there.
And the "House of Prayer" is no further away
Than the quiet spot where you kneel to pray.
For the heart is a temple when God is there,
As we place ourselves in His loving care.

And He hears every prayer and answers each one,
When we pray in His Name, "Thy Will Be Done."
And the burdens that seemed too heavy to bear,
Are lifted away on "The Wings of Prayer."

—Helen Steiner Rice

(Reprinted by permission of Gibson Greeting Cards, Inc.)

"Do you not know or have you heard? The LORD is the eternal God, creator of the ends of the earth. He does not faint or grow weary, and his knowledge is beyond scrutiny. He gives strength to the fainting; for the weak he makes vigor abound. Though young men faint and grow weary, and youths stagger and fall, they that hope [wait] in the LORD, will renew their strength, they will soar as with eagles' wings; they will run and not grow weary, walk and not grow faint" (Isa. 40:28-31).

Take time to *think* of God and His Son Jesus, who are the source of power. Take time to *read the Word of God daily;* it is the fountain of wisdom. Take time to *pray;* it is the greatest communication you can have with the eternal God. Take time to *accept Jesus* as your *loving Saviour and Lord of your life,* for this is the *key to Heaven.*

CHAPTER IV

When I entered the Convent at eighteen, I came to realize very quickly that I was still quite human. The fact that I knew Jesus personally eased the situation, but I had never really been disciplined in my life. For four years before becoming a nun, I had been living practically on my own and following Jesus pretty easily—without any parental supervision. Then came a rugged road that only Jesus' love made victorious. I needed His love to overcome the desires of the flesh. Circumstances I had never encountered before presented themselves. God was teaching me how I could learn to deny myself, take up my cross, and follow His Son, Jesus Christ.

We all need His love to make the road of life straight and less rocky in order to travel safely to our final destination.

Man was created for love; he is a reflection of God's enduring and merciful love. Yet, true love is neither possessive nor binding. Truly, God does not force men in any way to return His love. I can remember Jesus saying in Scripture, "Here I stand knocking at the door. If anyone hears me calling and opens the door, I will enter his house and have supper with him, and he with me" (Rev. 3:20).

We discover that divine love blooms like a flower that unfolds in spring. As a man woos his fiancee, so God woos us. His love is manifested every second of the day and every day of the year. God promises His followers a love that never changes, a security that never collapses, and a peace no man can take from us.

Yet, since nearly the dawn of creation, man has been running away from God. "When they heard the sound of the LORD God moving about in the garden at the breezy time of the day, the man and his wife hid themselves from the LORD God among the trees of the garden" (Gen. 3:8).

Pride caused the downfall of Lucifer. Disobedience marred most generations after Adam. Jealousy caused the first death in history. Wickedness produced the first flood during Noah's time. The spirit of independence caused God to bring confusion to the ones who were constructing the Tower of Babel. Ungodliness buried the two cities of Sodom and Gomorrah.

Yet, the majority of men, seemingly intelligent creatures, never learn how they can avoid the pitfalls. And so today men still blame God for wars but lose sight of the greed and selfishness of nations that really cause them. Men still blame God for sickness and death, yet forget that these have been caused by Adam's sin of disobedience. Men still blame God for the world's economic, social, and moral degradation, but are too blind to see men's independence and self-righteousness as the reasons for it.

"When we put on our prized robes of righteousness we find they are but filthy rags. Like autumn leaves we fade, wither and fall. And our sins, like the wind, sweep us away. Yet no one calls upon your name or pleads with you for mercy. Therefore you have turned away from us and turned us over to our sins.

"And yet, O Lord, you are our Father. We are the clay and you are the Potter. We are all formed by your hands. Oh, be not angry with us, Lord, nor forever remember our sins. Oh, look and see that we are your people" (Isa. 64:6-9, TLB).

Of all the enemies we think we have, our own selfishness is the greatest. It robs us of peace within, joy in our hearts, and the security we all need in these disturbing times. Selfish love reminds me of an apple that is red and shiny and delicious to look at, but within is the worm that gnaws and eats the heart of the fruit. It is not detected by others at first sight, and in our own blindness, we never see it.

Selfishness works havoc in anyone's life. It produces *fear*—fear of not being accepted by our acquaintances, fear of being laughed at or ridiculed when we speak out our convictions, fear of losing our jobs when competition faces us, fear of not being able to provide for ourselves and our loved ones, fear of suffering when we are told of a malignant disease, fear of death, judgment, the unknown, and on and on.

Fear primarily causes *worry,* and it steals from us the time, the strength, and the talents God has given us to use for His honor and glory. We usurp from God the gifts of mind and use them for our own self-destruction. We are *trusting ourselves* rather than God, the God Who is well able to lead us on to a victorious life.

Godly love of self, on the other hand, is entirely different. It desires discipline of oneself, self-development of one's talents and other potentialities for the service of God and others. It also reminds us to keep our bodies fit for the indwelling of the Holy Spirit. Such things as proper exercise, sufficient sleep, eating the right foods (balanced diet), abstaining from nicotine, excess caffeine, and overeating are all ways to discipline our bodies.

This true love of self produces the fruit of the Holy Spirit such as love for God and others, joy, peace, patience, endurance, kindness, generosity, faithfulness, gentleness, and self-control.

Some years ago, a paralyzing fear crept into my life. It was lodged in my unconscious mind, and from time to time it would emerge. As it is with most people's fears, there was no logical reason for mine. Living in a religious community, I had all the temporal security one could wish for in this life. Yet, I visualized that someday I would be forced to work for my living. Never ever having had a permanent job before I entered the convent, I had a false notion that I was incapable of securing one.

It all ended one day when I visited a church not of my own denomination. Before the end of the service, the minister suggested that anyone in the congregation who had any fears could be released from them that very hour. I quickly realized that I had one and gave it over to Jesus as the minister suggested.

From that time on, I was delivered from the fear.

This deliverance was a precious gift from God, for not many years after, I joined a new Community that is self-supporting. Only once did the fear return, and I quickly renounced it in the name of Jesus Christ, and it was gone. "The Spirit God has given us is no cowardly spirit, but rather one that makes us strong, loving, and wise. Therefore, never be ashamed of your testimony to our Lord" (2 Tim. 1:7-8).

God wants no fear in our lives. He wants us to turn all our fears over to Him. "Perfect love casts out all fear. And since fear has to do with punishment, love is not yet perfect in one who is afraid" (1 John 4:18).

"I say to you *who are My friends:* Do not be afraid of those who kill the body and can do no more. I will show you whom you ought to fear. Fear him who has the power to cast into Gehenna [hell] after he has killed. Yes, I tell you, fear him. Are not five sparrows sold for a few pennies? Yet not one of them is neglected by God. In very truth, even the hairs of your head are counted! FEAR NOTHING, then. You are worth more than a flock of sparrows" (Luke 12:4-7, emphasis mine).

The United States is one of the most prosperous nations in the world. God blessed its very conception, because He came first in the founding of our purpose of life, liberty, and the pursuit of happiness. What has happened over the past two hundred years? Though we are still a generous nation, does it excuse us for the selfishness we find in the majority of our homes, small businesses, large corporations, and the whole industrial and political setup?

One of the latest outward signs of the increasing godlessness in this country is an organization called "The American Humanist Association." This group calls for a new direction for mankind, stressing a belief in his so-called "rational powers" and criticizing theistic religion as an impediment to human development.

Humanism puts the self at the *center* of everything, completely negating the concept of God-centered spiritual commitment.

We may be shocked at such a philosophy, but I wonder how many of us in the United States live as if Christianity were a myth instead of a reality?

The TV commercials give us an insight to some of the results of our materialistic and self-centered philosophies: some advertisements are for digestion and heartburn—remedies to relieve the symptoms of overeating—others are for tranquilizers to relieve and reduce tension, and still others are for a seemingly endless number of gadgets and timesavers to make life more comfortable for us.

None of these things can satisfy our desire for the happiness and love we need in our lives. It would be wonderful to simplify our lives by just trusting God and leading the Christ-centered life which would free us from petty strivings. Then we could reach out and obtain His love and be concerned for others, for His sake.

"Yes, all have sinned; all fall short of God's glorious ideal; yet now God declares us 'not guilty' of offending him *if we trust in Jesus Christ,* who in his kindness freely takes away our sins" (Rom. 3:23-24, TLB).

An intelligent church-going woman asked me recently, "If Jesus died for our sins, why do we still have them?" This question is a good example of how some people have never been instructed in their churches. Peter teaches us in his first letter, "In his own body he [Jesus] brought your sins to the cross, so that all of us, dead to sin, could live in accord with God's will. By his wounds you were healed. At one time you were straying like sheep, but now you have returned to the Shepherd, the Guardian of your souls" (1 Pet. 2:24-25).

Most people believe and trust in their intellect. They believe Jesus is God, that He became man, died for their sins and rose again, but their life is not controlled by God. One must repent from his worldly and selfish sins, turn completely around from self, and accept Jesus as his Saviour and Lord of his life.

Jesus became my Saviour at the early age of seven when I accepted His death on the cross for punishment for all my sins. I experienced a personal encounter with Him, and from then on I *knew* He loved me. I realized that He would have died just for my sins, His love for me was so great. He loves you, also, in the very same way.

To accept Jesus as the Lord of my life was another concept. I recognized His Kingship over me as I grew older and became a teenager. I then accepted His creative power in me. In return, I wanted to love Him and bend my will into His in every detail and circumstance in my life. In other words, He became my everything! He is my Lord and Saviour! Praise God! He can be yours, too, TODAY. Accept Him into your heart, acknowledge your sins, confess to the world that He is your Lord and Saviour of your life, and you can conquer the world, the flesh, and the devil!

Our lives are transformed only when we accept Jesus and give Him priority over everything and everyone. The control of self without the help of Jesus and the Holy Spirit utterly fails, even though we may think we are religious, church-going people. Our acts of self-denial, routine pious devotions, or participation in external ceremonies in church cannot change a person spiritually. We must have a personal relationship with Jesus. In other words, we must be "born again" inwardly.

The only way to follow the teachings of Jesus is to make a decision to give up self and let Him take over. Jesus calls ALL PEOPLE to Himself when He says, "If ANYONE wishes to come after me, he must deny his very self, take up his cross and begin to *follow in my footsteps.* Whoever would save his life will lose it, but whoever loses his life for my sake *will find it*" (Matt. 16:24-25).

Jesus said you should take up your cross willingly and follow HIM. This indicates that a Christian will not have all "pie in the sky" in this life. He must face reality. Circumstances will bring sorrows and trials, but we do have a loving Lord Who cares about and loves us. Praise God!

IT MATTERS TO ME ABOUT YOU

My child, I know thy sorrows, thine every grief I
     share;
I know how thou art tested, and, what is more—I care.

Think not I am indifferent to what affecteth thee;
Thy weal and woe are matters of deep concern to Me.

But, child, I have a purpose in all that I allow;
I ask thee then to trust Me, though all seems dark just
     now.

How often thou hast asked Me to purge away thy
     dross!
But this refining process involves for thee—a cross.

There is no other pathway if thou would'st really be
Conformed unto the image of Him Who died for thee.

Thou canst not be like Jesus till self is crucified;
And as a daily process the cross must be applied.

Just as the skillful gard'ner applies the pruning knife,
E'en so, I too would sever the worthless from thy life.

I have but one sole object—that thou should'st fruit-
     ful be!
And is it not thy longing that I much fruit should see?

Then shrink not from the training I needs must give
     to thee;

I know just how to make thee what I would have thee
    be.

Remember that I love thee! Think not I am unkind,
When trials come to prove thee, and joy seems left
    behind.

'Tis but a little longer until I come again;
What now seems so mysterious will all be then made
    plain.

Take courage then; and fear not! Press forward to the
    prize,
A crown of life awaits thee, glory before thee lies!

—Alice C. Lefroy

In the course of counseling many married couples, I find that both parties need *sacrificial love*—
first, in their communications with each other and,
secondly, in their sexual relationships. Selfish love,
self-interest, and a strong self-will are the main reasons why so many marriages fall apart. The example
of Jesus' love must penetrate into their own personal
lives. They cannot give what they do not possess.

Married life becomes a life worth living when
each party realizes his or her shortcomings and both
develop the power to conquer their problems. This
can only be accomplished when they receive strength,
insight, and love from a personal relationship with
Jesus and through reading His Word.

Peter, who was a married man, gives very good

counsel to any married person who is really in earnest. He says, "You married women must obey your husbands, so that any of them who do not believe in the word of the gospel may be won over apart from preaching, through their wives' conduct.

"They have only to observe the reverent purity of your way of life. The affectation and elaborate hairdress, the wearing of golden jewelry, or the donning of rich robes is not for you. Your adornment is rather the hidden character of the heart, expressed in the unfading beauty of a calm and gentle disposition. This is precious in God's eyes. The holy women of past ages used to adorn themselves in this way, *reliant on God* and *obedient to their husbands*—for example, Sarah, who was subject to Abraham and called him her master. You are her children when you do what is right and let no fears alarm you.

"You husbands, too, must show consideration for those who share your lives. Treat women *with respect* as the weaker sex, heirs just as much as you to the gracious gift of life. If you do so, *nothing will keep your prayers from being answered*" (1 Pet. 3: 1-7).

Jesus sums it up for all of us when He says, "Be compassionate as your Father is compassionate. Do not judge, and you will not be judged. Do not condemn, and you will not be condemned. Pardon, and you shall be pardoned. Give, and it shall be given to you. Good measure pressed down, shaken together, running over, will they pour into the fold of your garment. For the measure you measure with will be measured back to you" (Luke 6:36-38).

When married couples do not find fulfillment in their union, a dangerous and sorrow-filled road lies ahead. This need not be if they *trust Jesus* and let Him take over the controls.

Another pitfall of sin, or selfish love, is the craving for ungodly sexual relationships. Some are willing to sell for a cheap price the precious temple that God has given them.

Teaching Harlem boys some years ago, I gave them an example of how degrading our bodies is sinful and demoralizing; a person not only destroys himself, defiling his God-given image, but also destroys others. All I had to mention was the place—42 and Broadway in New York City, and they all knew to what I was referring.

Our society has reached a new low in its moral behavior, from living in common law marriages to husband and wife swapping. Much of the so-called civilized culture of the United States has degenerated into paganism. Nothing can demonstrate this better than the increase in homosexual and lesbian practices. The saddest part of the situation is that some religions are accepting the above conditions and establishing the rationale that they still should be admitted into society as sinless.

The only solution some religions give these people is to see a psychiatrist. Man cannot save man! Morally, we have gone back to the time of Sodom and Gomorrah.

"These men who exchanged the truth of God for a lie, worshipped and served the *creature* rather than the *Creator*. God therefore delivered them up to disgraceful passions.

"Their women exchanged natural intercourse for the unnatural, and the men gave up natural intercourse with women and burned with lust for one another. Men did shameful things with men and thus received in their own persons the penalty for their perversity. They did not see fit to acknowledge God, so God delivered them up to their own depraved sense to do what is unseemly.

"They are filled with every kind of wickedness: maliciousness, greed, ill will, envy, murder, bickering, deceit, craftiness. They are gossips and slanderers, they hate God, are insolent, haughty, boastful, ingenious in their wrongdoing and rebellious toward their parents.

"One sees in them men without conscience, without loyalty, without affection, without pity. They know God's just decree that all who do such things deserve death, yet they not only do them but approve them in others" (Rom. 1:25-32).

No person can be set free from his sin until he is made to feel his own slavery. But trying to save ourselves is as hopeless as the plight of a man who has fallen into a frozen pond with no one in sight.

Saving us is a task that only Jesus, the Son of God, can accomplish. "Those who live according to the flesh are intent on the things of the flesh. . . . The tendency of the flesh is toward death, but that of the Spirit toward LIFE AND PEACE. The flesh is at enmity with God; it is not subject to God's law. Indeed, it cannot be; those in the flesh cannot please God. If you live according to the flesh, you will die; but if by the Spirit you put to death the evil deeds of the body, you will live" (Rom. 8:5-8, 13).

Jesus told us that everyone who lives in sin is a slave of sin. That is why, if the Son, Jesus, frees you, you will be really free. "I AM the Way, and the Truth, and the Life" (John 14:6).

God has given us intellect to use, *not* for our own self-destruction or selfish interest and gains, but to build up the potentials of everyone for the kingdom of God, to enlighten those in darkness by way of the truth. When we depart from the Source of our intellect, we lose so much of what the majority of people are searching for—peace of mind and the joy that fills the heart.

When the mind is flooded with everything but the truth, it can only be confused and in an endless search for interior peace. Many who are always searching and studying are never able to reach the knowledge of truth. Today, we have thousands of young people who want to expand their minds with eastern mysticism, dope, LSD, and the like.

If only they knew the depth, the wisdom, the expansion of the mind that can be obtained by knowing the Person of Jesus and His Word. "If you live according to my teaching, you are truly my disciples; then you will know the truth, and the truth will set you free" (John 8:32). "The wages of sin is death, but the gift of God is eternal life in Christ Jesus our Lord!" (Rom. 6:23).

There are two extreme forms of selfish love. One is self-perfection and the other, suicide. The former clings to self in a tantalizing state of inward blindness, groping for light but always turning inward in self-analysis. The suicidal person gives up even the thread of hope for existence. Each in his own way trusts himself and is unable to find enlightenment or comfort.

Suicides are not always psychotic, but often are poor souls caught up in a web of loneliness, self-pity, alcoholism, and/or drug addiction. The inability to communicate and a feeling of isolation are among the reasons for suicides today. Another, and more logical, reason is that so few know others they can trust among their own circle of friends. In losing the feeling that there is meaning in his life, the person falsely assumes that there is no one to whom he can turn.

But Jesus stretches out His hand and says, "The Son of Man has come to search out and save what was lost" (Luke 19:10). How Jesus longs for our friendship. We can never be lonely or feel isolated when we have Jesus. He is truly our Best Friend in all situations of life. "Do not let your hearts be troubled. Have faith [trust] in God and faith in me" (John 14:1).

Jesus knew what the conditions would be today. Through the Holy Spirit, Paul wrote, "There will be terrible times in the last days. Men will be lovers of self and of money, proud, arrogant, abusive, disobedient to their parents, ungrateful, profane, inhuman, implacable, slanderous, licentious, brutal, hating the good. They will be treacherous, reckless, pompous, lovers of pleasure rather than of God as they make pretense of religion but negate its power. Stay clear of them" (2 Tim. 3:1-5).

How wonderful to know that those who are

seeking Jesus can find help; those who trust Him will always have a Divine Hand outstretched to lift them out of the mire, or out of the guilt feelings we have all experienced. How Jesus longs to be our security, our peace and hope in these last days. Trust Jesus and He will come to you. *"Everyone* who calls on the name of the Lord will be saved" (Rom. 10:13).

I'll run my own life! Have you heard that expression before? With good health, college degrees, and financial security, people imagine they do not need God's help. They say, "God has given me an intellect to solve any problems and difficulties that arise." And so, they blindly face life by themselves. In following their own self-will, they soon learn that confusion follows. As the mouse rotates in circular motion within his cage, so people with selfish aims create lives without purpose or meaning.

I'm reminded of a famous movie star who thought she could go it alone, as so many do. Her problems started when she found her life was not vital to herself or to anyone else. Then she married, thinking that this would fill the void and solve the problem. Giving herself completely to her husband and his wishes, she gave up her movie career and her former friends. In time, her emptiness became apparent; she was emotionally and physically drained. Finally, the marriage broke up.

She relates, "I told God I didn't know which way to turn, so I wanted Him to show me the way. I prayed, 'Take over my life, because I've messed it up.' And God did. It was just beautiful! Step by step, little by little, I was let out of darkness. I saw a whole new and better world open up for me."

Today, many men and women of all professions are turning from themselves, their frustrations and emptiness, and giving their lives over to Jesus Christ. And, oh, what an exchange! Instead of an unfulfilled life of selfish love, they find a full and overflowing rich life in Jesus, where He purifies and nourishes them in His love. "I AM the way, and the truth, and the Life." "Apart from me you can do nothing" (John 14:6 and 15:5).

If we could only learn what God told the prophet years ago, "Cursed is the man who trusts in human beings, who seeks his strength in flesh, whose heart turns away from the LORD. He is like a barren bush in the desert that enjoys no change of season, but stands in a lava waste, a salt and empty earth.

"Blessed is the man who trusts in the LORD, whose hope is the LORD. He is like a tree planted beside the waters that stretches out its roots to the stream: It fears not the heat when it comes, its leaves stay green; in the year of drought it shows no distress, but still bears fruit. More tortuous than all else is the human heart, beyond remedy; who can understand it? I, the LORD, alone probe the mind and test the heart, to reward everyone according to his ways, according to the merit of his deeds" (Jer. 17:5-10).

Man's pride and self-will causes him not only to have a life without divine purpose, but also to have a life that is fruitless for himself and others. You know, O Lord, that man is not master of his fate. Man's course is not within his choice, nor is it for him to direct his steps. "Let not the wise man glory in his wisdom, . . . but rather, let him who glories, glory in this, that in his prudence he knows me" (Jer. 9: 22-23).

Many a naturally good person sees no reason why he should conform to God's will. Not being able to look into the future, he does not realize the consequences of a self-ruled life, even one filled with good works for others. Matthew 7:21 states that only those who do the will of the Father will enter the Kingdom of God. The wisdom of this world is absurdity with God, as Paul says, "He catches the wise in their craftiness. The Lord knows how empty are the thoughts of the wise" (1 Cor. 3:19-20).

You do not have to be afraid that God will take away your personality when you give up your will to Him. All individuals are unique. God wishes you to become a whole person in all aspects: physically, mentally, and spiritually. When you give your will to Him, He is able to cleanse and purify you, so that your life may become filled with His peace, joy, and love.

Jesus explained this to the woman at the well when He said, "EVERYONE who drinks this [natural] water will be thirsty again." So it is with our human endeavors. No matter what we do in good works and activities, we still remain human and thirst for His love. But, "whoever drinks the water [pure spiritual nourishment] I give him will never be thirsty; no, the water I give shall become a fountain within him, leaping up to provide eternal life" (John 4:13-14).

Our lives become transformed as we surrender our wills and let His will take over. There cannot be any identity crisis when you follow Jesus. He makes all things new in you. "I AM the vine, you are the branches. He who lives in me [through repentance and acceptance of Jesus] and I in him, will produce abundantly, for apart from me you can do nothing" (John 15:5).

One of the greatest failings in natural man is the sin of racial hatred, with its accompanying sins of prejudice, unforgiveness, bitterness, and revenge. It actually causes tension in the mind, along with distress to the physical body. It corrodes the heart and destroys communication and relationships with others. Everything may be all right when we are with our own—in our own homes, social circles, and the like. But just introduce, for example, the topic of a black person moving into the neighborhood or receiving the job one thinks he should have; then we discover what is really inside our hearts and minds, how far removed we are from observing God's injunction, "You shall love your neighbor as yourself" (Matt. 22:39).

Jesus made it more potent when He said, "I give you a new commandment: love one another. Such as my love has been for you, so must your love be for each other. This is how all will know you for my disciples; your love for one another" (John 13:34-35).

The primary cause of prejudice is our lack of the knowledge that we have ALL SINNED. "If we say that we have no sin [for example, racial hatred, prejudices, unforgiveness, or revenge], we are only fooling ourselves, and refusing to accept the truth. If we claim we have not sinned, we are lying and calling God a liar, *for he says we have sinned"* (1 John 1:8, 10, TLB).

In the model prayer, "The Our Father," Jesus teaches us we will not have our sins forgiven unless we forgive everyone and let go of our racial hatred, prejudices, unforgiveness, bitterness, and revenge. Could we ever suffer from our enemies as Jesus suffered? He hung suspended on the Cross in agony and yet prayed for His enemies, "Father, forgive them; they do not know what they are doing" (Luke 23: 34).

Let us humble ourselves before God and look at the whole picture of our own pettiness. Compare it to the injustices that were bestowed on the sinless man, Jesus. All of us need to forgive and love one another as He did. With the natural man this is impossible, but with God helping us, all things are possible.

"You have been called to live in freedom—but not a freedom that gives free reign to the flesh. Out of love, place yourselves at one another's service. The whole law has found its fulfillment in this one saying: 'You shall love your neighbor as yourself.' If you go on biting and tearing one another to pieces, take care! You will end up in mutual destruction!

"My point is that you should live in accord with the SPIRIT and you will not yield to the cravings of the flesh" (Gal. 5:13-16).

CHAPTER V

God has the whole world in the palm of His hand. Do you trust Him with your life?

All through history, different empires have risen and fallen. This does not seem strange when we know that Satan has been the ruler of this world since the time of Adam. "Woe to you, earth and sea, for the devil has come down upon you. His fury knows no limits, for he knows his time is short" (Rev. 12:11).

There is but one nation that has survived them all! A look into the past will reveal why these unusual happenings have occurred.

It was in the Garden of Eden that the first *promise* of redemption was given, as Genesis 3:15 records. Notwithstanding the great sinfulness of man, God's love overpowered the punishment. Once more, in the time of Noah, man turned against God. In His mercy, He spared eight "just" people and gave them a covenant through the rainbow, a *promise* that He would never permit a flood to devastate the world again. Genesis 9:11-14 gives this account.

There were few on earth who worshipped the one true God. In time, He would form a nation that

that would reveal to everyone His great love and His almighty power.

Abraham was called to be the father of that nation. God appeared to him and said, "I am the Almighty; obey me and live as you should. I will prepare a contract between us, guaranteeing to make you a mighty nation. In fact you shall be the father of not only one nation, but a multitude of nations!" (Gen. 17:2-4, TLB). *God promised* them a land of their own if they would love, obey, and trust Him.

Seventy Israelites, the family of Jacob, moved to Egypt because of a famine in Canaan. God continued to form them into a nation during the four hundred years they remained in Egypt. The Lord fully intended them to return to their promised land, but His ways were not their ways. No doubt the Israelites would have forgotten their agreement with God if they had lived a prosperous and contented life in Egypt. So often we forget God when things are going smoothly.

As it happened, the Israelites became so numerous in Egypt that they were commanded to become slaves. God saw their extreme suffering. "I have seen the deep sorrows of my people in Egypt, and have heard their pleas for freedom from their harsh taskmasters" (Exod. 3:7, TLB).

Time and time again, God reminded them of His loving concern. He was their only God to be worshipped in spirit and in truth. "Hear, O Israel! the LORD is your God, the LORD alone! Therefore, you shall love the LORD, your God, with all your heart, and with all your soul, and with all your strength.

Take to heart these words which I enjoin on you today" (Deut. 6:4-6).

God never changes! After thousands of years He still waits and longs for our love. How few hear His voice and respond. But for those who do, what a tremendous and glorious life of victory awaits them, now and forever.

There is no other way! I know many people who do not look for the promises of God in the Bible. They complain and grumble about everything and then expect the blessings of God. Their lack of faith and trust are stumbling blocks that prevent the flow of love and the abundance of gifts God wishes to bestow on them.

God wants our whole heart, mind, soul, and strength. Unfortunately, the Israelites turned their eyes toward false gods, even after seeing the mighty miracles God performed for them.

Do not be too hasty to judge the Hebrews. After two hundred years in our own wonderful America, is there not a parallel? Are we not spinning toward destruction, when we, too, trust everyone and everything but the Lord? "The fool says in his heart, 'There is no God.' Such are corrupt; they do abominable deeds; there is not one who does good. God looks down from heaven upon the children of men to see if there be one who is wise and seeks God" (Ps. 53:1-2).

Moses, the Israelites' leader, reminded them before entering the promised land of Canaan, "In all history, going back to the time when God created man upon the earth, search from one end of the heavens to the other to see if you can find anything like this. Where else will you ever find another example of God removing a nation from its slavery by sending terrible plagues, mighty miracles, war, and terror? He did these things so you would realize that the Jehovah is God, and that there is no one else like him" (Deut. 4:32, 34-35, TLB).

Moses prophesied the following in God's name, "In the future, when you have been in the land a long time, and you have defiled yourselves by making idols, and the Lord your God is very angry because of your sin . . . you shall be quickly destroyed from the land. Jehovah will scatter you among the nations, and you will be but few in number" (Deut. 4:25, 27, TLB).

"But you will also begin to search again for Jehovah your God, and you shall find him when you search for him with all your hearts and souls. When those bitter days have come upon you in the latter times, you will finally return to the Lord your God and listen to what he tells you. For the Lord your God is merciful—he will not abandon you nor destroy you nor forget the promises he has made to your ancestors" (Deut. 4:29-31, TLB).

There was a wonderful reason for this chosen race to be formed. Jesus Christ, the Anointed One, was to fulfill the first covenant in order to establish the second. He said, "Sacrifice and offering you did not desire, but a body you have prepared for me. Holocausts and sin offerings you took no delight in. Then I said, 'As it is written of me in the Book, I have come to do your will, O God' " (Heb. 10:5-7). The Hebrew nation did not need to be surprised by the coming of Jesus. Over three hundred details of His life and ministry were predicted hundreds of years earlier.

The first one was foretold in Genesis 3:15-16 in the Garden of Paradise. Centuries later, God spoke to Moses, "I will raise up for them a prophet like you from among their kinsmen, and will put my words into his mouth; he shall tell them all that I command him. If any man will not listen to my words which he speaks in my name, I myself will make him answer for it" (Deut. 18:18-19).

This prophecy was fulfilled in the life of Jesus. John's Gospel records it. Jesus said, "Whoever rejects me and does not accept my words already has his judge, namely, the word I have spoken—it is that which will condemn him on the last day" (John 12: 48).

"Anyone who loves me will be true to my word, and my Father will love him; we will come to him and make our dwelling place with him. He who does not love me does not keep my words. Yet the word you hear is not mine; it comes from the Father who sent me" (John 14:23-24).

Here are a few of the prophecies in the Old Testament concerning Jesus' birth on earth of a virgin mother. "Therefore the Lord himself will give you this sign: the virgin shall be with child, and bear a son, and shall name him Immanuel" (Isa. 7:14).

He was to be born in a specific location. "But you, Bethlehem-Ephrathah, too small to be among the clans of Judah, from you shall come forth for me one who is to be ruler in Israel; whose origin is from

81

of old, from ancient times" (Micah 5:1).

The amazing life continues with the Massacre of the Holy Innocents. "Thus says the LORD: In Ramah is heard the sound of moaning, of bitter weeping! Rachel mourns her children, she refuses to be consoled because her children are no more" (Jer. 31: 15). And Jesus' return from Egypt, when He was still a boy is also prophesied, "When Israel was a child I loved him, out of Egypt I called my son" (Hosea 11:1).

When His forerunner, John the Baptist, prepared the way for Jesus' public life, it recalled the *prophecy* of Isaiah, "A voice cries out: In the desert prepare the way of the LORD! Make straight in the wasteland a highway for our God" (Isa. 40:3).

The early public life of Jesus relates His reading the scripture of Isaiah in the synagogue. "The spirit of the Lord GOD is upon me, because the LORD has anointed me; He has sent me to bring glad tidings to the lowly, to heal the brokenhearted, to proclaim liberty to the captives and release to the prisoners" (Isa. 61:1). "Today, this Scripture passage is fulfilled in your hearing" (Luke 4:21).

Jesus' triumphal entrance into Jerusalem was recorded much like a historical happening. Zechariah 9:9 proclaims, "Rejoice heartily, O daughter of Zion, shout for joy, O daughter of Jerusalem! See, your king shall come to you; a just saviour is he, meek and riding on an ass, on a colt, the foal of an ass."

One can see the many prophecies of Jesus' passion portrayed in the various accounts in the Old Testament writings. Among them are Isaiah, chapters 50 and 53, and the following Psalms of David: 34, 22,

41, and 69. Jesus predicted His own death and burial, but always with the knowledge that there would be victory over death. Psalm 16:9-11 prophesies it in the Old Testament.

"It is in Christ and through his blood that we have been redeemed and our sins forgiven, so immeasurably generous is God's favor to us. He has put all things under Christ's feet and has made Him, thus exalted, head of the church, which is his body: the fullness of him Who fills the universe in all its parts" (Eph. 1:7, 8, 22-23).

But the story of the Jewish nation was not finished. Jesus knew His love would be rejected: "To his own he came, yet his own did not accept him" (John 1:11).

Later, when Jesus rode triumphantly into Jerusalem, "He began to cry. 'Eternal peace was within your reach and you turned it down,' he wept, 'and now it is too late. Your enemies will pile up earth against your walls and encircle you and close in on you, and crush you to the ground, and your children within you; your enemies will not leave one stone upon another—for you have rejected the opportunity God offered you' " (Luke 19:42-44, TLB).

This prophecy was fulfilled on September 26, in the year 70 A.D. Titus, the Roman emperor, captured the last stronghold, the "Upper City" in Jerusalem, and the Roman Empire reigned.

Today, in these latter times, Jesus' prophecy has come to pass already. He said, "Jerusalem will be trampled by the Gentiles, *until the times of the Gentiles are fulfilled"* (Luke 21:24).

It was not only at this time, during the Roman invasion, that the Jewish nation was under captivity. It started during the reign of the Babylonian Empire, 586-537 B.C. Then came the Persian rule of domination from 537-332 B.C. The Greek-Hellenistic rule over Israel followed, 332-142 B.C. During the life of Jesus, the Jews were in bondage to the Roman-Byzantines, 4-614 A.D. The Arabs also had a ruling power in Israel from 648 to 1099 A.D.

The sad experience of the crusades rule lasted from 1099-1291 A.D., followed by the Nameluke rulers of Egypt, 1291-1516 A.D. The Ottoman dynasty, which fell into the hands of the Turks from 1516 to 1917, had at first a period of Oriental culture. In the 19th century, the European culture became dominant. After the upheaval caused by the fighting in the First World War, 1914-1917, Palestine became a British Mandate.

It was in the "last days of the Ottoman Empire that the idea prevailed of return to the Promised Land—an idea that impelled several thousands of emancipated young Jewish people to leave the confines of their eastern European ghettos. 1878 A.D. saw the foundation of the first agriculture settlement at Pitah-Tiqva, today a town of 100,000 people in the suburbs of Tel Aviv. Until that time, small Jewish populations located themselves in just the four traditionally holy cities of Jerusalem, Hebron, Safed and Tiberias."[1]

Another return of Jews to Palestine that was notable was the advent of political Zionism in 1897. "After 1900, the immigrants no longer arrived in small groups, but in thousands."[2] Tel Aviv was founded in 1909 and is today a city of about 600,000.

"The second movement followed the Russian revolution in 1905, mostly immigrants from Russia and Poland."[3]

"The third wave of immigration followed the First World War and the setting up of the British Mandate. Before 1930, the Jewish population in Palestine was only 50,000. [Prominent in the Renaissance, figured the Hebrew language, which had been in virtual oblivion for two thousand years.] "[4]

"The fourth wave of immigration after 1933 brought 60,000 Jews from Germany and central Europe in flight from the Nazi regime."[5]

I mention the above immigrations, not as a thing in passing, but in preparation for what God *promised* the Hebrew nation thousands of years ago. The state of Israel, founded in 1948, received more than a million and a half immigrants, mostly refugees from Europe, North Africa, and the Near East. All this was foretold by God's prophet in Ezekiel 36: 19-21. "I scattered them [the Jews] among the nations, dispersing them over foreign lands; according to their conduct and deeds I judged them. But when they came among the nations (wherever they came), they served to profane my holy name, because it was said of them: 'These are the people of the LORD, yet they had to leave their land.' So I have relented because of my holy name which the house of Israel profaned among the nations where they came."

And verse 24 continues, "I will take you away from among the nations, gather you from all the

foreign lands, and bring you back to your own land."
More than three million Jews from over one hundred
countries have re-entered Palestine.

The second prophecy concerns the reclamation
of the ruined land. "Therefore, prophesy concerning
the land of Israel, and say to the mountains and the
hills, the ravines and valleys: Thus says the Lord God:
with jealous fury I speak, because you have borne the
reproach of the nations. Therefore do I solemnly
swear that your neighboring nations shall bear their
own reproach. As for you, mountains of Israel, you
shall grow branches and bear fruit for my people Israel, for they shall soon return" (Ezek. 36:6-8).

The third prophecy was the rebuilding of the
ruined cities, Beersheba, Ashdod, Ashkelon, Jaffa,
Kiryat-Gat, Dimona, and Arad, to name a few. "I will
settle crowds of men upon you, the whole house of
Israel; cities shall be repeopled, and ruins rebuilt. No
more will I permit you to bear the reproach of nations, or bear insults from peoples, or rob your people of their children, says the Lord GOD" (Ezek. 36:
10, 15).

"I will bring about the restoration of my people
Israel; they shall rebuild and inhabit their ruined cities, plant vineyards and drink the wine, set out gar-
dens and eat the fruits. I will plant them upon their
own ground; never again shall they be plucked from
the land I have given them, say I, the LORD, your
God" (Amos 9:14-15).

The fourth prophecy concerns the binding of
the former two kingdoms of Israel and Judah together.
God spoke through the prophet, saying, "I will take

the Israelites from among the nations to which they have come, and gather them from all sides to bring them back to their land. I will make them *one nation* upon the land, in the mountains of Israel, and there shall be one prince for them all. Never again shall they be two nations, and never again shall they be divided into two kingdoms" (Ezek. 37:21-22, emphasis mine).

The fifth prophecy, which is now being accomplished, is the fulfillment of the rebuilding of the Temple. "My dwelling shall be with them; I will be their God, and they shall be my people. Thus the nations shall know that it is I, the Lord, who make Israel holy, when my sanctuary shall be set up among them forever" (Ezek. 37:27-28).

God describes, through the prophecy of Ezekiel, that a nation from the north shall come in war against the Jewish nation. The Lord God says, "You are the one I spoke of long ago through the prophets of Israel, saying that after many years had passed, I would bring you against my people. But when you come to destroy the land of Israel, my fury will rise! For in my jealousy and blazing wrath, *I promise a mighty shaking in the land of Israel on that day.*

"All living things shall quake in terror of my presence; mountains shall be thrown down; cliffs shall tumble; walls shall crumble to the earth. I will summon every kind of terror against you, says the Lord God, and you will fight against yourselves in mortal combat. I will fight you with sword, disease, torrential floods, great hailstones, fire and brimstone. Thus will I show my greatness and bring honor upon my name, and all the nations of the world will hear what

I have done, and know that *I am God!*" (Ezek. 38: 17-23, TLB, emphasis mine).

The Old Covenant that brought about the Hebrew nation is finished. The Old Law was brought about by Moses, but enduring love and grace came through Jesus Christ.

God's fulfillment of His PROMISES AND PROPHECIES throughout history is absolute proof of His authenticity and reliability. He is still ALIVE and READY to meet your every need, if you but accept Him, love Him, and trust Him with your life.

What He has done in the past, for the saints in the Old and New Law, He will do for you. Your eternal life has been bought already by Jesus' death on the cross. You have only to receive it in faith. The promises of God are for you and me today! I have found them to be so true in my own life. As a child, His promises of true love and friendship were my support. "Those who love me I also love, and those who seek me find me (Prov. 8:17).

"God has said, 'I will never desert you, nor will I forsake you.' Thus may we say with confidence: 'The Lord is my helper, I will not be afraid; what can man do to me?' " (Heb. 13:5-6).

The Old Testament (including the Psalms, Proverbs) and the Gospels in the New Testament are filled with promises that God has given us.

My "King's Insurance Policy" is a good proof that God can and does keep His promises in a very practical way. There are promises for housewives, business men and women, mothers, children, servants, teenagers, laborers, and all professional people. Seek them in Scripture, trust Him and see for yourself. We have not only today to live in victory, but a wonderful future that God promised, also.

John the Apostle writes in the Book of Revelation that he heard a loud voice in heaven saying, "Now have salvation and power come, the reign of our God and the authority of his Anointed One. For the accuser of our brothers is cast out [Satan], who night and day accused them before our God. They defeated him by the *blood of the Lamb* and by the *word of their testimony;* love for life did not deter them from death" (Rev. 12:10-11).

We have yet to wait for the parousia (the rapture). My prayer is that the Christian who knows Jesus personally will stand firm and TRUST GOD AND HIS WORD and avoid compromise with the world, the flesh, or the devil, despite the persecutions and the threats that prevail. We are to wait patiently for the fulfillment of God's mighty promises of the future. "The heavens and the earth will pass away but my words will not pass" (Matt. 24:35).

Everyone who is a true practicing Christian will welcome God's words, "Remember I AM COMING SOON! I bring with me the reward that will be given to each man as his conduct deserves. I AM the ALPHA and the OMEGA, the First and the Last, the Beginning and the End. Happy are they who wash their robes so as to have free access to the tree of life and enter the city through its gates! Outside, the dogs [all those who are uncircumcised in the heart—the Jews call all the uncircumcised, dogs] and sorcerers, the fornicators and murderers, the idol-worshipers and all who love falsehood. . . . The Spirit and the Bride say, 'COME!' LET HIM WHO HEARS ANSWER, 'COME.' Let him who is thirsty come forward; let all who desire it accept the gift of life-giving water" (Rev. 22:12-15, 17, emphasis mine).

1. Michael Avi-Yonah, "The Holy Land," *Park and Roche Establishment* (Schaan, 1972), Reprinted by permission of Holt, Rinehart and Winston, p. 224.

2. Ibid., p. 233.

3. Ibid., p. 239.

4. Ibid.

5. Ibid.

CHAPTER VI

The majority of people living in the United States do not realize how easy it is to practice idolatry. It seems to be such an old-fashioned word—only found in former cultures and practiced years ago. But what does it mean in today's language? According to one definition in Webster's dictionary, an idol is an object of excessive devotion!

That statement causes us all to think, doesn't it? Just *what* or *who* claims our thoughts and interest all day? What do we think about at daybreak, something to pull us through into evening? Could it be that we do not have our lives in proper perspective as to true values.

If we do not call on God for help, we are in danger of being controlled by other beings more powerful than ourselves. Some who do not believe and trust in God search for alternatives in their desperation. They want immediate help in their situations.

Many feel the established religions have failed them, and they seek refuge and counsel elsewhere. Impetuous people sometimes seek short cuts to fame and fortune. Others want to escape the fetters of their own senses. Sheer boredom urges some to look for entertainments and thrills. Loneliness, caused by bereavement, leads others to trust in ways that can ruin their lives physically, mentally, and morally.

There are many means and practices which people rely on and trust in today, ways they think will solve their problems and difficulties and let them take a look into the future. They participate and become involved in one or more of various ideologies such as astrology, ouija boards, hypnosis, ESP, card reading, fortune telling, pendulum, séances, spiritualism, divination, witchcraft, modern psychics, magic arts, etc. These have been practiced for thousands of years and have manifested an evil supernatural power which is superior to man's natural abilities. They have been and are used for business endeavors, social activities, educational helps, recreational pastimes, and religious teachings outside the Christian life.

I remember a teenage girl who lived in the same little California town I did many years ago. She attended Catholic school and out of curiosity went to the gypsies to have her fortune told—just for fun! Months later she took her own life, carrying out her future as they had foretold. What power made her follow the directions that were against self-preservation?

In teaching women prisoners in New York City, I have come across many women who killed either their own children or parents because they heard a voice telling them to do it. What power beyond their control led them to commit an action beyond human understanding?

For centuries man has wondered, as you must have wondered, why there is so much sickness, crime, destruction, and death in this world.

The natural man can achieve scientific feats such as going to the moon; he can accomplish technological efficiency and intellectual status that stagger the mind of the average person. Yet, the natural man cannot extinguish the hate, greed, and racial prejudice that prevail in our world today. Society has not solved the alcohol and drug problems or eliminated the urge to kill or rape. Why is man so powerless?

The natural man, the worldly and selfish person, cannot gain victory over a spiritual power he thinks does not exist. If he knows but does not acknowledge the power of God, if he will not perceive and confess the cleansing power of the blood of Jesus and will not let Jesus control his life, he will in no way master the invisible forces that control the world today.

The Word of God states, "We are not fighting against people made of flesh and blood, but against persons without bodies—the evil rulers of the unseen world, those mighty satanic beings and great evil princes of darkness who rule this world; and against huge numbers of wicked spirits in the spirit world" (Eph. 6:12, TLB).

The problem of sin started with invisible beings. It continues today. Let us turn back the pages of time and read, "The LORD has established his throne in heaven, and his kingdom rules over all. Bless the LORD, all you his angels, you mighty in strength, who do his bidding, obeying his spoken word. Bless the LORD, all you his hosts, his ministers, who do his will" (Ps. 103:19-21).

What a blessed privilege to have had God's friendship and to have been in His company where peace and love reigned. But pride and disobedience lurked in Lucifer, and through his rebellion, "war broke out in heaven; Michael and his angels battled against the dragon. Although the dragon and his angels fought back, they were overpowered and lost their place in heaven.

"The huge dragon, the ancient serpent known as the devil or Satan, the seducer of the whole world, was driven out; he was hurled down to earth and his minions with him. . . . But woe to you, earth and sea, for the devil has come down upon you! His fury knows no limits, for he knows his time is short" (Rev. 12:7-9 and 12:11).

The writings of Isaiah state, "How you are fallen from heaven, O Lucifer, son of the morning! How you are cut down to the ground—mighty though you were against the nations of the world. For you said to yourself, 'I will ascend to heaven and rule the angels. I will take the highest throne. I will preside on the Mount of Assembly far away in the north. I will climb to the highest heavens and be like the Most High.'

"But instead, you will be brought down to the pit of hell, down to its lowest depths. Everyone there will stare at you and ask, 'Can this be the one who shook the earth and the kingdoms of the world? Can this be the one who destroyed the world and made it into shambles and demolished its greatest cities and had no mercy on his prisoners?' " (Isa. 14:12-17, TLB).

Lucifer and his followers were condemned to hell. Jesus stated, "I watched Satan fall from the sky like lightning" (Luke 10:18). God did not spare even the angels who sinned, but threw them into hell, according to 2 Peter 2:4. And Matthew 25:41 explains that everlasting fire was prepared for the devil and his angels.

When God finished the creation of the earth, and the first man and woman were formed, Satan was standing by waiting to tempt them.

God has given every human being free will, and every person is tested; just as Adam and Eve were tempted in the garden, so we are tempted today.

We all know the story of how God tested our first parents and what happened as the result. Through the fallen angelic spirits, sin, pain, and death entered our world. Cain was guilty of the sin of jealousy, and it led him to commit a greater sin, murder (Gen. 3 and 4). "Once passion has conceived, it gives birth to sin, and when sin reaches maturity, it begets death" (James 1:15).

Thousands of years later, Jesus warned unbelievers against the wiles of the devil, "Why do you not understand what I say? It is because you cannot bear to hear my word. The father you spring from is the devil, and willingly you carry out his wishes. He brought death to man from the beginning, and has never based himself on truth; the truth is not in him. Lying speech is his native tongue; he is a liar and the father of lies" (John 8:43-44).

Father John Nicola, Assistant Director of the National Shrine in Washington, D.C., says the devil's greatest weapon is the belief that he does not exist, "The Spirit distinctly says that in the latter times some will turn away from the faith and will heed deceitful spirits and things taught by demons" (1 Tim. 4:1).

At times, Christians and non-Christians alike find themselves suffering physically, mentally, or emotionally from spiritual oppression. These miseries may be caused by satanic attacks. Anything that destroys peace of mind, such as confusion, doubts, fears, depression, hatred, etc., is not from God. Mental illness is never from God, but from the forces of evil and destruction.

Jesus said, "The thief comes only to steal and slaughter and destroy. I came that they might have LIFE and have it to the FULL. My sheep hear my voice. I know them, and they FOLLOW ME. I give them ETERNAL LIFE, and they never perish" (John 10:10, 27-28). Most people are not aware that their misfortunes could stem from their being or having been involved in some form of witchcraft at some period in their lives. It is also possible that any involvement in such things by their parents could affect the children.

A Christian couple I knew on the East coast suffered from demonic persecution, even though they had both dedicated their lives to the spreading of God's Word and had trusted and relied on Jesus in every aspect of their lives. But both had parents who had practiced witchcraft, primarily spiritualism, and they were affected by it.

The husband had been institutionalized several

times and finally through instruction, and through the prayer and fasting of friends, found relief. No sooner was he freed, than his wife developed serious mental problems to the extent that she attempted suicide. She was sent to a hospital and, after a very severe crisis and much prayer, came out alive. Thank God, in Jesus' Name, there has been no reoccurrence of the onslaughts by the evil spirits.

The most common and sly practice that has crept into our modern society is the widespread belief in and dependence on astrology, as evidenced by the horoscope columns in over a thousand daily newspapers. Many people who supposedly worship God on Sunday will not do anything on a weekday without first consulting their personal chart or the horoscope column in the paper.

"When you look up to the heavens and behold the sun or the moon or any star among the heavenly hosts, do not be led astray into adoring them and serving them. Take heed, therefore, lest, forgetting the covenant which the LORD, your God, has made with you, you fashion for yourselves against his command an idol in any form whatsoever (Deut. 4:19, 23).

It is estimated that in the United States alone there are 5,000 astrologers that chart the heavens for over 10 million Americans who earnestly follow and trust in them. The popularity of astrology these days reflects the weakening of faith and even reason among the people.

"He [Jesus] is the image of the Invisible God, the first-born of all creatures. In him everything in heaven and on earth was created, things visible and invisible . . . all were created through him, and for him. . . . In him everything continues in being" (Col. 1:15-17).

Years ago, I saw ouija boards displayed in a window of a well-known department store in San Diego. Very appropriately a mannequin, dressed as a devil, was selling them. My high school students doubted me when I told them that the devil was the author of these things. Knowing they were playing with them at home, I invited a student to bring one to class to prove my point.

I asked the questions as they played it. It answered all the inquiries even the last one, "Where does the person come from who is doing the writing?" Big letters spelled out "HELL." We cannot remain long in God's friendship and participate in anything that takes His place.

Besides taking pills to keep awake for academic studies and examinations and other pills to make them sleepy, some students now resort to self-hypnosis to obtain good marks. This takes away the free will God gave them, so they can absorb the subject matter. The academic degree is the first priority in their lives, not God.

"Every young man who listens to me and obeys my instructions will be given wisdom and good sense. Yes, if you want better insight and discernment, and are searching for them as you would for lost money or hidden treasure, then wisdom will be given you, and knowledge of God himself; you will soon learn the importance of reverence for the Lord and of trusting him.

"For the Lord grants wisdom! His word is a treasure of knowledge and understanding. He grants good sense to the godly—his saints. He is their shield, protecting them and guarding their pathway" (Prov. 2:1-8, TLB).

Many have heard of the late Episcopal Bishop James A. Pike and his involvement in spiritualism in his attempts to communicate with his deceased son (a suicide). Since then, it has become a favorite pastime for many San Franciscans. One man in that city was brought to us for instructions on how to free himself from his bondage.

He could neither eat nor sleep. He naively became involved and realized afterward that he was trapped in a web that was beyond his human power to escape. After instructions, prayer, and fasting, he was freed, but he was forced to move from his apartment building because it had become saturated with evil spirits.

There are many people who in good faith, but through lack of instruction, do not realize the difference between truth and error. These people are searching for the truth and unfortunately meet with organizations such as Rosicrucian, Spiritualist, Mormon, Christian Science, Unity, Bahai, Theosophy, Inner Peace Movement, Spiritual Frontier Fellowship, Association of Research and Enlightenment, Religious Research Foundation of America, Unitarian, Jehovah's Witness, Krishna Consciousness, and Scientology, etc.

All the above occult societies *deny* in their

teachings that Jesus Christ is the Divine Son of God. Jesus does not have priority in their lives, but some other philosophical ideal, person, or thing fills His place. This mistaken allegiance opens the door to oppression by the power of darkness.

"Don't always believe everything you hear just because someone says it is a message from God: test it first to see if it really is. For there are many false teachers around, and the way to find out if their message is from the Holy Spirit is to ask: Does the teaching decree that Jesus Christ, God's Son, became man with a human body?" (1 John 4:1-2, TLB).

Satan is very well aware that all knowledge comes through the mind. This is the reason that in these last days there is such widespread interest in the development of psychic research. There is a great acceptance of parapsychology as a science, of hypnotism by psychiatrists and the medical profession, and of ESP and other mind-control courses such as the Silver Method (man's name). These practices can even be found in some Catholic schools, convents, and retreat houses.

Jean Dixon, Uri Geller, Miki Dahne, Edgar Cayce, Arthur Ford, and Ruth Montgomery are famous psychics who predict the future outside of God's will. But God says, "There shall not be found with you anyone that uses fortune telling, soothsayer, or magician, a witch, or hypnotist, or medium or a clairvoyant or psychic or a spiritualist. For all these things are an abomination to the Lord" (Deut. 18:9-12).

Another false teaching that has become popular

is Transcendental Meditation, "T.M." It has attracted many well-known people in the United States, not to mention a large segment of the spiritually hungry youth culture. The initial ceremony (costing from $35 and up) includes an offering of fruit and flowers placed before the picture of the *swami* in an incense-laden candlelit room. There is the "laying on of the hands" and a secret word (a mantra) given to the devotee which he chants silently until "cosmic consciousness" is achieved.

Because the founder (modern exponent) Maharishi Mahesh Yogi (who received widespread publicity when the Beatles rock group from England paid him a visit in India) does not proclaim it as a religion, many have tried to teach and practice it in our school system in the U.S.

Any mind-control system, no matter what it is called, is directly opposed to the teachings of Jesus Christ, WHO is the center of Christianity. He said, "I AM the WAY, and the TRUTH, and the LIFE; no one comes to the FATHER but through ME" (John 14:6)—not through cosmic consciousness!

If modern man could only grasp the truth that JESUS IS THE ANSWER for all pure meditation, if through our minds and hearts we could surrender our wills and our lives to God our Father, we could then meditate on His WORD, His LIFE. Then Jesus could bring (free of charge) the supreme love and goodness of God into our daily living.

His Holy Spirit never plays a double part; He tells the TRUTH of the cost of our salvation—the blood, sufferings, and death of Jesus on the cross.

When we accept His love, He shows us the cost of sacrificing our own will. Too many people would rather "play religion" through "T.M." or play Sunday church in keeping the Old Law or do their own thing rather than come face to face with the reality of God's teachings in the Bible.

Saint Paul was put in prison with Silas, his colleague, because of a demon-possessed slave girl. She was a fortune teller and kept shouting, "These men are servants of God and they have come to tell you how to have your sins forgiven." This went on day after day until Paul in great distress turned and spoke to the demon within her. "I command you in the name of Jesus Christ to come out of her." Instantly, it left her. "Her masters' hopes of wealth were now shattered; they grabbed Paul and Silas and took them before the judges at the market place" (Acts 16:17-19, TLB).

It makes no difference in what century you live. No one can be a victorious Christian without getting rid of this attachment to all forms of witchcraft as soon as the Holy Spirit speaks to him.

"Many of the believers who had been practicing black magic confessed their deeds and brought their incantation books and charms and burned them at the public bonfire. This indicates how deeply the whole area was stirred by God's message" (Acts 19:18-20, TLB).

In ancient years, in the early Church, or today, cruelty has been the outstanding characteristic in the worship of the devil and his cohorts. Sacrificing children by fire to the false gods was practiced by the heathen nations before Christ, and cruelty is still prevalent among satanic groups of people. Scripture depicts Satan as a fowler (one who traps wild fowl), a wolf, a roaring lion, and an old serpent. And the ones who succumb to Satan are those who *willingly* remain in ignorance—persons out of fellowship with God, persons led astray by curiosity, and those who fail to read the Word of God and practice it.

One of the devil's main targets is the home. It is his desire to breed hatred, suspicion, and arguments right in our homes. If he can separate the members of a family through selfishness, pride, contention, rebellion, and lies, he has won his victory.

The evil spirits of infirmity might also try to rob you of your physical healing. Do not be fooled by the enemy. A year after I was miraculously healed of degenerative arthritis of the spine, satanic spirits attacked my spine, and I had to resort to crutches all that day. I did not realize where the difficulty came from. As I prayed in the evening, I recalled God was not a God of contradiction. He had healed me! The next morning my spine was normal again.

I have been attacked physically many times since then in many parts of my body, but I claim the victory with the following words, "In the name of Jesus Christ and through His precious blood, I demand the spirit of infirmity to leave my body. Amen." There are times when I repeat it and use other scriptures on healing. I will not stop praying until the victory is mine.

Jesus died to set me free of all physical, mental, and spiritual maladies. His victorious resurrection power and His precious blood can gain victories for you, too, in many ways. I know this through experience.

One example of this power was seen one day when I was in a post office in Manhattan. A lady was trying to purchase stamps but was unable to do so due to the screaming and kicking of her son. I realized the situation and softly said, "In the name of Jesus and His precious blood, I *bind* the spirits in that boy." Immediately, the boy stopped and later walked out of the post office with his mother as a normal boy. Hallelujah!

Homosexuality (and lesbianism), which I mentioned in an earlier chapter, is a sin and not a quirk of the mind as many doctors proclaim. This was verified by the scripture I quoted from the first chapter in Paul's letter to the Romans. The law that was passed recently in California condoning homosexuality is certainly a victory for Satan and will strengthen his attacks against our younger generation.

Americans and other people do not realize that Satan, who is the destroyer of life, claps his hands with glee every time an unwanted pregnancy is aborted. Irreverence for life, including taking the life of a fetus, of a handicapped person, of the elderly or the terminal patient, is irreverence for God.

Another technique the devil uses is the promotion of a society where drink and drugs are a prerequisite for social acceptance. He also leads numerous young couples into unnecessary debts, just to keep up with the Joneses.

Jesus said, "A man may be wealthy, but his

possessions do not guarantee him life" (Luke 12:15).

The devil, being very cunning, never reveals his intention to destroy your home, marriage, job, or your self-respect as a creature of God. Never feel you are safe enough in your own strength, that you do not need God's protection against the wiles and onslaughts of the tempter. "My fear is that, just as the serpent seduced Eve by his cunning, your thoughts may be corrupted and you may fall away from your sincere and complete devotion to Christ" (2 Cor. 11:3).

"Your strength must come from the Lord's mighty power within you. Put on all of God's armor [you must put it on—God won't do it for you] so that you will be able to stand safe against all strategies and tricks of Satan.

"For we are not fighting against people made of flesh and blood, but against persons without bodies— the evil rulers of the unseen world, those mighty satanic beings and great evil princes of darkness who rule this world; and against huge members of wicked spirits in the spirit world.

"So use every piece of God's armor to resist the enemy whenever he attacks, and when it is all over, you will be standing up.

"But to do this, you will need the strong belt of *truth* and the breastplate of *God's approval*. Wear shoes that are able to speed you on as you preach the Good News of peace with God. In every battle you will need *faith* as your shield to stop the fiery arrows aimed at you by Satan. And you will need the helmet of *salvation* and the sword of the Spirit—which is the

Word of God" (Eph. 6:10-17, TLB).

If, however, you are a victim of the devil's tactics, don't be discouraged. With God's help, together with the precious blood of Jesus and the power of the Holy Spirit, you can be freed by:

1. your confession of faith in Jesus Christ
2. confession of the occult sin
3. the renunciation of Satan
4. the command for Satan to depart.

Jesus gave all believing Christians power over our enemy, the devil, when He said, "I have given you power to tread on snakes and scorpions [when in precarious circumstances] and all the forces of the enemy [Satan], and nothing shall ever injure you" (Luke 10:19).

We must realize that every practicing Christian (one who has a God-controlled life) has this power, if he knows and trusts God's Word. For over two years I worked at the "soup kitchen" at Dorothy Day's Catholic Worker. During this time, five days a week, going back and forth to my apartment, I travelled the streets of skid row in the Bowery in New York City and was never once mugged or attacked.

In the soup kitchen itself, there was *never* a fight among the men while I was there in person. Why? I took God's promises literally. Besides praising God while I worked, I would also say in between times, *"In the Name of Jesus, I bind ALL the evil spirits that are here."* It worked!

In exceptional cases where oppression is severe and faith is weak, it may be advisable to have another Christian, strong in his faith, exorcise these powers of darkness, after the first three steps have been taken by the oppressed person.

All life is a spiritual warfare against the world, the flesh, and the devil. Peter warns us, "Stay sober and alert. Your opponent the devil is prowling like a roaring lion looking for someone to devour. Resist him, solid in your faith [trust and reliance on God]" (1 Pet. 5:8).

If we are to be victorious in all the circumstances of life, we must no longer cower before Satan, but must reckon with him as a defeated foe. We must realize once and for all that according to God's Holy Word, the devil's rights have been cancelled. He tries to keep us in ignorance of the resurrection power that Christ has given us through the Holy Spirit. "Greater is He that is in you, than he that is in the world" (1 John 4:4, KJV).

It is the resurrection power that makes us more than conquerors. Our victory in every circumstance of life is nothing more nor less than an amen of Faith to the great all-comprehensive victory that Christ finished at Calvary on our behalf.

It was for our sake that He came to champion our hopeless cause. The resurrection power that the Lord gives enables us to do the impossible things. Every time we come across an insurmountable task or an unbearable burden, He is prepared to reveal His resurrection power that makes all impossibilities possible.

Recently, I was introduced to a woman in church who looked like a living human vegetable. We prayed for her and many members of the church persevered in praying for her deliverance. She had been a Christian but, through the devil's tactics, had become the mistress of a man for three years.

Then the spirit of condemnation attacked her; she realized her sin, and a guilt complex settled upon her, but not toward conviction or repentance. Many times she tried to take her own life, but failed. Through the blood of Jesus, His resurrection power, and His Word in Scripture, she is today a model of joy and thanksgiving for her new life in Jesus because He conquered that spirit within her and accepted her repentance.

We sometimes think God is unkind to us when He permits us to face trials or temptations from the evil one, such as people we can't tolerate or conditions we cannot stand. These conditions are allowed in order to help us learn to trust our precious Saviour more and to call upon Him and His resurrection power to obtain the victory. Our prayer is that you might know Jesus and the power of His Holy Spirit. I do not speak from the experience of a day, but from the experience of a lifetime. The secret of victory is in total dependence and trust in the power of Jesus.

Christ proclaims, "I am the way and the truth and the life; no one comes to the Father but through me" (John 14:6).

In very simple words, if we do not belong to Jesus, the Son of God, we have committed ourselves to the enemy, Satan. There is NO MIDDLE ROAD! The lack of peace in your heart and mind is the prompting of the Holy Spirit to come to Jesus and repent. Only when we rest in Jesus can we have peace in our whole being: heart, soul, mind, spirit, and emotions. Our physical, intellectual, and spiritual life can then be renewed. True self-love surrenders all to Jesus and rejects the world, the flesh, and the devil!

"I am the gate. Whoever enters through me will be safe. He will go in and out, and find pasture. The thief [the devil] comes only to steal and slaughter and destroy. I came that they might have life and have it to the full" (John 10:9-10).

CHAPTER VII

Have you ever needed a friend? One you could talk to and express what was in your heart without having it telegraphed to the whole world?

As a little girl growing up, I often needed and wanted a friend. Oh, yes, I had a mother and a father, but dad had such a disposition that no one ever returned after their first visit. I also had two older sisters, but who wants a little kid sister, nine or ten years younger trailing after them. Then mother died when I was fourteen!

Many of you have had worse situations, more problems in your family than I ever had. Who did you go to? What did you do during those formative years as a child? Have your wounds of resentment, fears, hate, etc., been healed over the course of years? Or have they grown deeper through bitterness, anger, or revenge for those who made you suffer?

Thank God, there was a Friend I met early in my childhood that brought me through every bitter experience, every heartache, every lonely hour. JESUS was that Friend, and He can be your Friend, too. No matter what your past was like or what the present offers, His Hand is outstretched to you NOW. His heart yearns to lift your burdens, warm your cold empty life with His love.

"In the beginning was the Word [Jesus], and the Word was with God, and the Word was God." John the apostle had known through experience that the Word was made flesh and dwelt among us, for he had seen and beheld His glory "as of the only begotten of the Father, full of grace and truth" (John 1:1, 14, KJV).

Jesus never intended this world to be a place of chaotic confusion, a battleground of greed, hate, violence, of dog eat dog. From the very first, God created this earth to be a vestibule of heaven, where man could walk with God in the cool of the day and the quiet of the evening.

It has been a long time since our first parents spoiled the picture. But God's love and Jesus' sacrifice still abound. How many of us have accepted His generous gifts?

Jesus has always been the eternal brightness of God's love, the expressed image of His Person. He forever upholds all things by the power of His Word. In time, Jesus purged our sins by dying on the cross and now sits at the right hand of the Father in glory and majesty.

How do I know He lives today? I experience His life within my heart!

If you have never known this wonderful personal relationship with the Word, Jesus will prove to you that He lives today, if you are sincere. "Jesus Christ is the same yesterday, today, and forever" (Heb. 13:8).

So many people in Jesus' time longed for Him to be King. He had all the qualities! He supplied all their needs!

Today, as well as yesterday, Jesus is not only the Word of God, but also the Bread of Life. How He tried to teach this message to the vast crowds years ago. But the majority of the people put the material, the tangible, substance before the spiritual. He reminded them again and again, "God is a Spirit: and they that worship him must worship him in spirit and in truth" (John 4:24, KJV).

Isaiah wrote God's thoughts when he penned, "This people draw near me with their mouth, and with their lips do honor me, but they have removed their heart far from me, and their fear toward me is taught by the precepts of men" (Isa. 29:13, KJV).

Jesus wants to be loved for Who He is and not for what He can give. This is the reason why Jesus has very few true friends even today. The reward He offers is very great, but there are few who want to pay the price for it.

Paul tells us that our attitudes should be like those of Jesus, "Let nothing be done through strife or vainglory [pride] ; but in lowliness of mind let each esteem others better than themselves." "Don't think just about your own affairs, but be interested in others, too, and in what they are doing" (Phil. 2:3-4, KJV-TLB).

Humility was the very first qualification that Jesus gave for being happy (blest) in this life in His Sermon on the Mount. You and I know that this is not what we find in the world today, either in business, educational trends, social customs, world trade, or in governments. Yet the paradox comes when we do humble ourselves.

Peter the apostle remembered the days when all of his colleagues were trying for the first place in the kingdom. Many times they were found arguing about who would be the greatest. It was through Peter's great sin of denial that he learned how weak he actually was. Later he wrote, "(You younger people), submit yourselves unto the elder. Yes, all of you be subject to one another, and be clothed with humility: for God resisteth the proud and giveth grace to the humble. Humble yourselves therefore under the mighty hand of God, that he may exalt you in due time" (1 Pet. 5:5-6, KJV).

Jesus not only gave us an example of humility at the Last Supper by washing the apostles' feet, but He warned them and us when He said, "Among the heathen, kings are tyrants and each minor official lords it over those beneath him. But among you it is quite different. Anyone wanting to be a leader among you must be your servant. And if you want to be right at the top, you must serve like a slave. Your attitude must be like my own, for I, the Messiah, did not come to be served, but to serve, and to give my life as a ransom for many" (Matt. 20:25-28, TLB).

Jesus, the Word of God, also gives humble, Spirit-filled Christians the same power and the same gifts as He Himself manifested on this earth. I believe there are many more spiritual needs in this world to be healed and tended to than there are physical ones.

As a social worker, counselor, etc., I find many

broken hearts. The fears and frustration of people are part of this world's playground. So many occupants are swinging back and forth, riding on a merry-go-round, never knowing where they are going.

Christians can give Jesus to the poor (either spiritually or financially poor), heal the broken-hearted, and mend their wounds of despair, depression, loneliness or discouragement. Through Christ's power Christians can bring deliverance to the captives (sinners held bound by Satan); recover sight to the blind (ignorant and non-instructed); and set at liberty them that are bruised (hurt by spiritual leaders, teachers, spouses or relatives and acquaintances who don't know Christ). These are what Christ did, according to Luke 4:18. God wants to heal the whole person!

As a little girl I remember the stained glass windows in church, showing Jesus healing the sick, feeding the poor, etc. I always knew that Jesus had the power, as God, to heal the sick and to create anything out of nothing. But I never realized He could do those wonderful things for me personally.

My first bout with pain was when I was four years old. My tonsils had to be removed! A few years later it was blood poisoning in my knee, which almost necessitated my leg to be amputated. A short time later it was the extraction of decayed teeth without any Novocain. And so it went.

After eight years of being a healthy sister in a traditional Order in California, another siege of physical pain hit me for twenty-five long years. This time it was spine trouble. It was always a continual surrender every time a new situation arose, due to the circumstances of the spine problem (especially when working seven days a week). For years this test of faith (my trust in God) had to grow, or else I would have been overwhelmed with doubts that God loved me, and eventually would have given in to bitterness, anger, frustration, and hatred toward God.

But I knew the Word! I knew Jesus personally, and I knew He loved me! For Jesus had said, "If you trust me, you are really trusting God. For when you see me, you are seeing the one Who sent me. I have come as a Light to shine in this dark world, so that all who put their trust in me will no longer wander in the darkness" (John 12:44-46, TLB).

It was poems like the following that also strengthened my faith in God.

PERFECT TRUST

Oh! for the peace of a perfect trust
My loving God, in Thee;
Unwavering Faith that never doubts
Thou choosest best for me.
Best, though my plans be all upset
Best, though the way be rough
Best, though my earthly store be scarce,
In Thee, I have enough.

Best, though my health and strength be gone,
Though weary days be mine,
Shut out from much that others have;
Not my will Lord, but Thine.
And e'en though disappointments come,

115

They, too, are best for me,
To wean me from this changing world
And lead me nearer Thee.

Oh! for the peace of a perfect trust,
That looks away from all,
That sees Thy Hand in everything,
In great events or small.
That heavenly Voice, a Father's Voice,
Directing for the best
Oh! for the peace of a perfect trust
A heart with Thee at rest.

After twenty-five years of pain, the unexpected happened. I was destined to be a bedridden patient from the degenerative arthritis of the spine. I was in traction morning and afternoon and could hardly manage to walk on crutches due to the protrusion of blood red muscles in my right leg. Neither could I sit in a wheelchair any longer.

At this time, as before, it was a complete surrender to God's will, but not without hope. It was through the Word of God that I found my answer. My Father's Word in the Bible had through the years been my support and encouragement.

Now, through the instruction of two Christian ladies, Jesus, the Divine Physician, was to heal me also. In two days I was miraculously healed in my own backyard, alone with Jesus. The next day it was confirmed by the fifth doctor who said I was a hopeless case. He examined me thoroughly, and I was dismissed that very day.

Some people will object to my enthusiasm over the Word of God. Others will say to themselves, I just can't understand it. The Scripture explains why: "God has actually given us His Spirit (not the world's spirit) to tell us about the wonderful free gifts of grace and blessings that God has given us. But the man who isn't a Christian can't understand and can't accept these thoughts from God, which the Holy Spirit teaches us" (1 Cor. 2:12, 14, TLB).

Others seem to have their minds and hearts covered by a thick veil. This veil of misunderstanding can only be removed by believing and trusting Jesus, not the world, the flesh, or the devil. When anyone turns to the Lord from his sins (repents), then the veil is taken away. The more one reads Scripture, the more he turns away from the spirit of the world. No man can serve two masters!

You ask me why I treasure the Word of God? *It taught me how to love others as Christ loves them.* The vertical love to God had been established when I was a child, but I was starved spiritually until I reached the time when I was fed daily in a *personal way* from Scriptures. This happened in 1940 when I began to read the Scriptures, meditate on them, and put them into practice on a daily basis. Today, I would like to share with you a "Well Balanced Spiritual Diet" which has helped so many people in their lives.

But first, let me give you a complete picture of what God has provided for us. He never intended that we should be miserable or unhealthy creatures on this earth. He loves us!

Even in the Old Testament God made hygienic laws concerning food—what to eat and what not to eat—in order that His people would remain healthy. See Deuteronomy, chapter 14.

Today, of course, we in United States and other countries are, so called, civilized people who have all the know-hows through technology. Yet we now have an avalanche of "junk food" that is not only causing hypoglycemia but cancer in many families, regardless of wealth or background.

Some of us then wonder why we can't think straight, work right, are overweight, have heart trouble, strokes, etc., but we don't realize we're not taking proper care of our diet.

Proper nourishment is one way to help us even have the pleasant dispositions we all should have as Christians. But eating, even the good foods, will never in itself make us happy, joyful, peaceful, or contented persons.

The reason is, as Jesus said, "Not on bread alone is man to live but on every utterance that comes from the mouth of God" (Matt. 4:4), and "I am the bread of life: he that cometh to me shall never hunger" (John 6:35, KJV).

Good food is very important in our life. We really can't live long without it. But spiritual food is even more necessary. You and I are working for food, shelter, pleasure, knowledge, maybe a new home, security, or promotion. All those are good in their proper places, but what about eternity? Can you and I ever get to heaven without Jesus?

"I am not ashamed of this Good News about

118

Christ. It is God's powerful method of bringing all who believe it to heaven. This message was preached first to the Jews alone, but now everyone is invited to come to God in this same way. This Good News tells us that God makes us ready for Heaven—makes us right in God's sight—when we put our faith and trust in Christ to save us. This is accomplished from start to finish by faith [trust in Jesus]. As the Scripture says it, 'The man who finds life will find it through trusting God' " (Rom. 1:16-17, TLB).

In my recent speaking tours, I found many who were helped mentally, emotionally, physically, and spiritually through the following *"well balanced spiritual diet"* which I recommended for *everyday* spiritual food.

Course 1. Read, "chew," and consume *two* or *three Psalms* a day (according to their length), beginning with no. 1 and continuing to the end.

Course 2. Read and "digest" *one Proverb* a day, according to the day of the month. Repeat monthly.

Course 3. Read and "masticate" *one or more chapters* in the *Old Testament,* beginning with Genesis and continuing through the O.T.

Course 4. Read and "assimilate" *one* or *less chapters* of the *New Testament,* beginning with Matthew. Repeat after the four Gospels are completed.

Course 5. Read and "absorb" *one chapter* of the *Acts of the Apostles*. Continue to the end of the Bible.

Repeat all courses!

Drinks. Drink all you want at the fountain of Living Waters, where Jesus refreshes the weary soul, "If any man thirst, let him come unto me, and drink" (John 7:37, KJV).

If anyone needs a Bible dictionary, one can obtain a paperback at any Christian bookstore. This diet is guaranteed to work toward the spiritual and physical health of all those who are placing their hope and trust in Jesus, the Rock of our Salvation.

We have, and do make, time for so many other activities in our lives. How about taking time to strengthen ourselves spiritually and mentally so we can obtain VICTORY over the world, the flesh, and the devil, and live like real Christians?

"The one who obeys me is the one who loves me; and because he loves me, my Father will love him; and I [Jesus] will too, and I will reveal myself to him" (John 14:21, TLB).

Many will think, as the rich man in the Bible did, we have plenty of time, all is well. Why bother about sharing with the poor and needy as the Word of God commands. But when death came, he was cast into hell. Being refused a small drop of water from Abraham, he asked about his brothers' futures who lived as he did. Abraham replied, "The Scriptures, the Word of God, have warned them again and again. Your brothers can read them."

"Oh! they won't bother to read them," the rich man in hell answered, "but if someone is sent from the dead they'll turn from their sins."

Abraham foresaw the future when he said, "If they won't listen to Moses and the Prophets, they won't listen to anyone even if they rise from the dead." Abraham's comments ring so true; Jesus did come back from the dead and how many do listen and obey?

Today, the Bible is the BEST SELLER but, I'm afraid, the least read on a *daily basis*. The worldly read their bible (the newspaper) faithfully! Can we be less fervent concerning "The Way" to Heaven? Let us not be foolish! We are dealing with eternal life!

Many times in the past I felt tempted to quit when the going was extremely rough. Fortunately, I thought of Jesus' words when He spoke to His apostles after many disciples left Him, "Will you also go away?"

And Peter replied, "Master, to whom shall we go? You alone have the words that give eternal life" (John 6:67-68, TLB).

What I have written about the Word is vividly illustrated through a dear friend of mine, Jenny. She was born and reared a Catholic, went to Church on Sunday, and kept all the Laws of God and the Church. But she admits her life was dull and drab even with a good husband and two beautiful children.

Then she met Jesus in a very personal way! Her life has not been the same since. From being a very shy, quiet person, she has blossomed into a beautiful mother who understands and loves her husband and children in a new way. Jesus is now teaching her through His Spirit of Love and Truth and by the Word of God.

Hunger for Scripture and relating it to others in a loving manner has created in her life a new interest, accompanied by an urge to help others in hospitals, etc., with a new understanding, compassion, and deep sympathy. She now attends the "Christians at Prayer" group in her Parish, where she fellowships with other growing Christians. Praise God!

Jesus told His followers at the Last Supper, "Let not your heart be troubled. You are trusting God, now trust in me. . . . If you love me, obey me; and I will ask the Father and he will give you another Comforter, and he will never leave you.

"He is the Holy Spirit, the Spirit who leads into all truth. The world at large cannot receive him, for it isn't looking for him and doesn't recognize him. But you do, for he lives with you now and some day shall be *IN YOU*. No, I will not abandon you or leave you as orphans in the storm—I will come to you" (John 14:1, 15-18, TLB).

How often people of this world rely on their own strength, their own intellectual abilities, and their financial resources to get ahead in life. They are always searching and seeking but never finding the fulfillment that satisfies the heart and mind. St. Augustine knew this through experience when he wrote, "Our hearts are restless, O Lord, until they rest in Thee."

Jesus is God, the Word made flesh Who dwelt

among us, yet He never attempted, as a human being, to start His public ministry until His baptism in the Jordan. The heavens then opened to Him, and He saw the Spirit of God coming down in the form of a dove, and He heard the voice from Heaven saying, "This is my beloved Son, and I am wonderfully pleased with Him" (Matt. 3:17, TLB). John the Baptist and the apostles baptized with water, but John said of Jesus, "He shall baptize you with the Holy Spirit and with fire" (Matt. 3:11, TLB).

Before Jesus' ascension into Heaven, He told His followers, "When the Holy Spirit has come upon you, you will receive power to testify about me with great effect" (Acts 1:8, TLB). The coming of the Holy Spirit on Pentecost Sunday made this tremendous power a reality. This was the beginning of the Church, not the end of that power!

Paul realized this when he proclaimed to the Corinthians, "I can never stop thanking God for all the wonderful gifts he has given you, now that you are Christ's: he has enriched your whole life. He has helped you speak out for him and has given you a full understanding of the truth; what I told you Christ could do for you has happened! Now you have every grace and blessing; every spiritual gift and power for doing his will are yours during this time of waiting for the return of our Lord Jesus Christ" (1 Cor. 1:4-7, TLB).

Countless numbers of Christians have had a real personal encounter with Jesus. Many, also, told me of their years of back-sliding. If the Holy Spirit guides and directs us, united with daily prayer and reading of His Word, there would be few that fall. Jesus knows our weaknesses, and in His love for us, He sends the Holy Spirit to reprove us of our sins against Him. It is God's Spirit who convicts us of our sins—sins of not trusting Him and sins against our neighbor—and He woos the sinner back through His great love.

Those who want to buy an orchard always identify the trees by their fruits. The same applies when one identifies a Christian. Jesus said, "You can tell their sincerity by their fruits."

When the Spirit controls our lives, He will produce a variety of good fruits, such as love (for God and neighbor), joy, peace, patience, kindness, goodness, faithfulness, gentleness, and self-control. If we live in the Spirit, let us also walk in the Spirit. We should keep away from pride, arguing, and irritating one another and we must refrain from that green-eyed monster of jealousy.

The following words tell us of God's wise plans to bring us into the glories of heaven. "Eye has not seen, ear has not heard, nor has it so much as dawned on man what God has prepared for those who love him. Yet God has revealed this wisdom to us through the Spirit. The Spirit scrutinizes all matters, even the deep things of God" (1 Cor. 2:9-10).

I pray, as Paul did, before the Father, from Whom every family in heaven and on earth takes its name, that He will bestow on you gifts in keeping with the riches of His glory. May God strengthen you inwardly through the working of His Holy Spirit. May *Christ dwell in your hearts* through *faith*, and may *love* be the root and foundation of your life. In this way, you will be able to grasp fully with all the saints, the breadth and length and height and depth of Christ's love, and *experience this love* which surpasses all knowledge so that you may attain to the fullness of God Himself.

The Holy Spirit, Whose power is now at work in you, can do immeasurably more than we dare ask or imagine. To God be the glory in the Church and in Christ Jesus through all generations, world without end.